HAMMOND **UNDERCOVER**™

KNIGHTS & WARRIORS

Published in the United States and its territories and Canada by
HAMMOND WORLD ATLAS CORPORATION
Part of the Langenscheidt Publishing Group

36-36 33rd Street, Long Island City, NY 11106

EXECUTIVE EDITOR: Nel Yomtov

EDITOR: Kevin Somers

Produced for Hammond World Atlas Corporation by

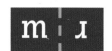

MOSELEY ROAD INC.
129 MAIN STREET
IRVINGTON, NY 10533
WWW.MOSELEYROAD.COM

MOSELEY ROAD INC.
PUBLISHER Sean Moore
ART DIRECTORS Brian MacMullen, Gus Yoo
EDITORIAL DIRECTOR Lisa Purcell

EDITOR Amber Rose
PHOTO RESEARCHER Ben DeWalt
DESIGNER Joanne Flynn
CARTOGRAPHY Neil Dvorak
COPYEDITOR Kate King
EDITORIAL ASSISTANTS Rachael Lanicci, Natalie Rivera

COVER DESIGN Linda Kosarin

Printed and bound in Canada

ISBN-13: 978-0843-708592

HAMMOND UNDER COVER™

KNIGHTS & WARRIORS

AARON RALBY

L HAMMOND World Atlas

Part of the Langenscheidt Publishing Group

Contents

Way of the Warrior

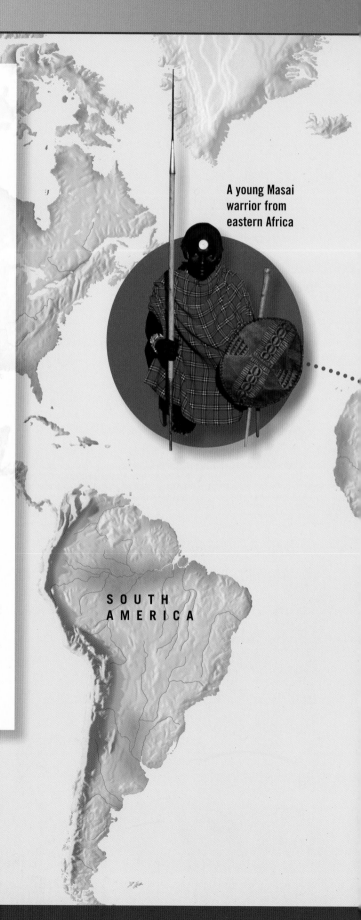

Throughout the globe, from east to west and north to south, the world of knights and warriors is a bloody one. In this book, we'll examine warriors from medieval and ancient history—before the use of guns and cannons—as well as those from later time periods. Warriors from many kingdoms and nations of Africa, the Americas, and the South Pacific used wooden, iron, and even stone weapons long after firearms were common in Europe. As you'll see, this sampling of warriors from around the world celebrates a warrior spirit common to all humankind.

Most people will agree that war is a terrible thing. It rips apart families and friends, ends lives early, and often brings out the worst in people. Despite all this, people have found something attractive in battle—otherwise, we would have stopped a long time ago!

Perhaps it is the qualities of a good warrior, a true hero, that we find so likeable: courage, strength, honor, and a willingness to die defending friends and family. If you really want to be a warrior, you will find that you can have these qualities without violence. Many traditions the world over have held that the true way of the warrior is one of peace. It is said that the best warriors are so good, they have no need to fight. Now, let's step back in time and begin our exploration of the ancient arts of battle!

A young Masai warrior from eastern Africa

SOUTH AMERICA

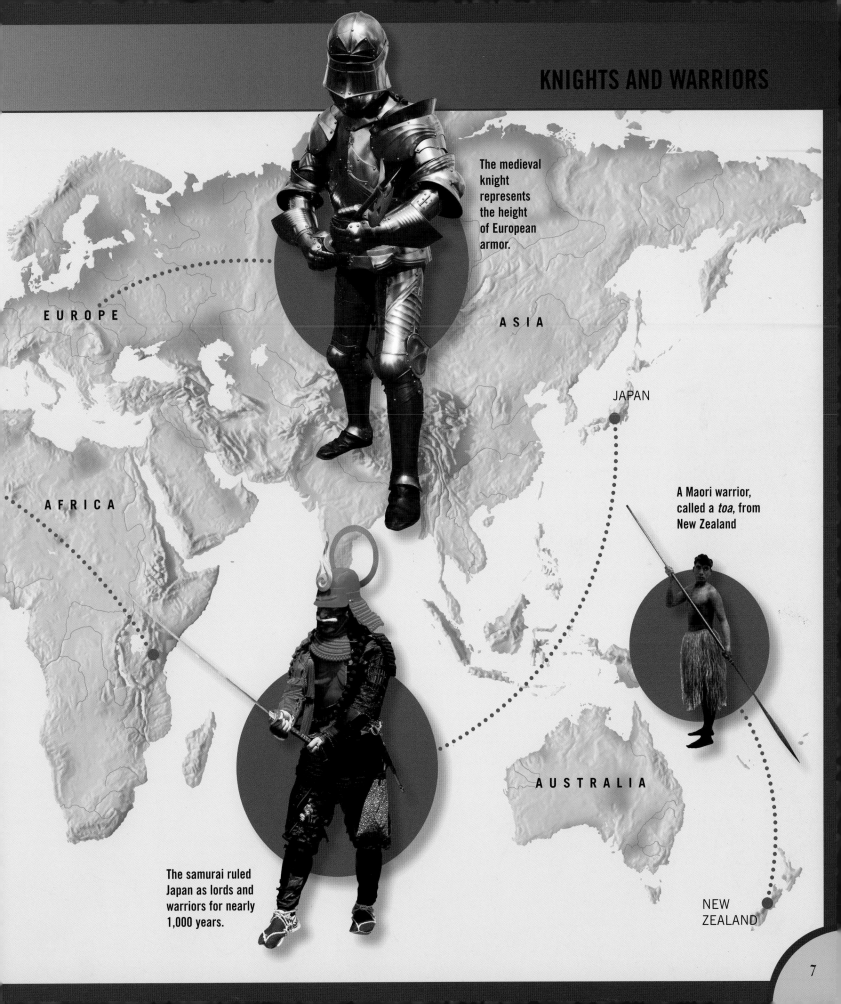

EUROPE

ASIA

AFRICA

JAPAN

AUSTRALIA

NEW ZEALAND

The medieval knight represents the height of European armor.

A Maori warrior, called a *toa*, from New Zealand

The samurai ruled Japan as lords and warriors for nearly 1,000 years.

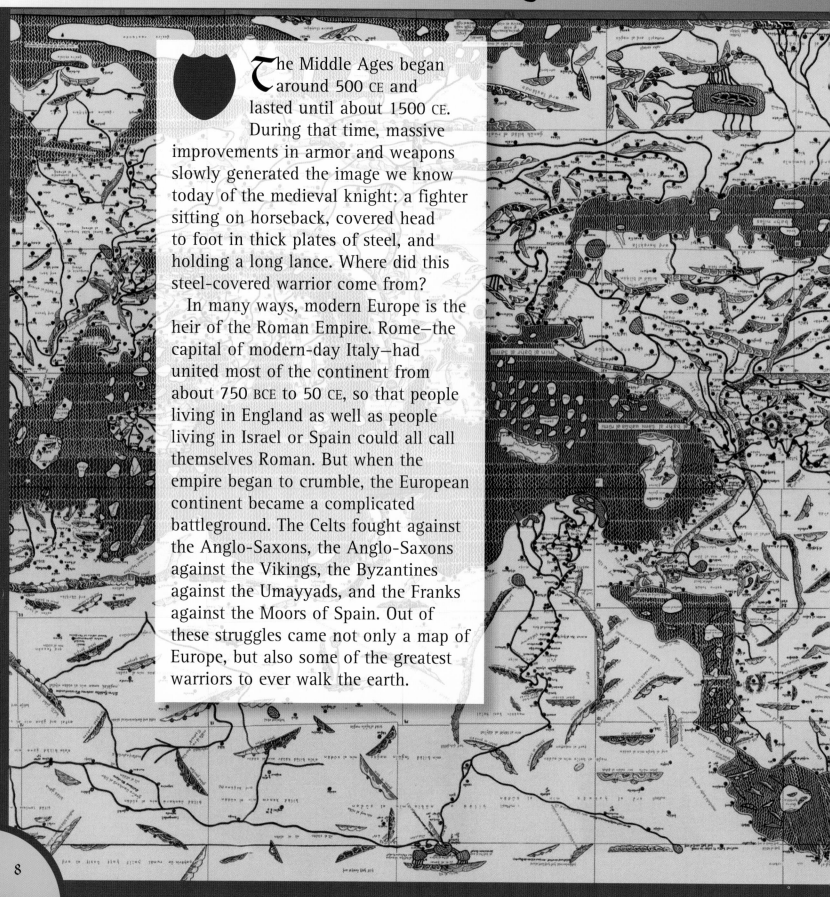

Warriors of the Dark Ages

The Middle Ages began around 500 CE and lasted until about 1500 CE. During that time, massive improvements in armor and weapons slowly generated the image we know today of the medieval knight: a fighter sitting on horseback, covered head to foot in thick plates of steel, and holding a long lance. Where did this steel-covered warrior come from?

In many ways, modern Europe is the heir of the Roman Empire. Rome—the capital of modern-day Italy—had united most of the continent from about 750 BCE to 50 CE, so that people living in England as well as people living in Israel or Spain could all call themselves Roman. But when the empire began to crumble, the European continent became a complicated battleground. The Celts fought against the Anglo-Saxons, the Anglo-Saxons against the Vikings, the Byzantines against the Umayyads, and the Franks against the Moors of Spain. Out of these struggles came not only a map of Europe, but also some of the greatest warriors to ever walk the earth.

From Empire to Ruin

The Middle Ages begin with the end of the Roman Empire. The fall of Rome is traditionally dated to 476 CE, but Rome didn't fall in a day! Instead, Roman traditions changed gradually over time, and sometimes didn't change much at all. In medieval Europe, Latin, the language of Rome, served as the common language.

At its height, the Roman Empire covered more than 2 million square miles—that's more than half of Europe. The Romans succeeded in building their empire in large part because of their superb military organization. Soldiers practiced working together in specific formations. The organization of the Romans allowed them to besiege cities and fortifications with shocking force. They developed numerous siege weapons (weapons designed for attacking fortifications), and the famous roads they built around Europe allowed them to control conquered territories with ease.

BRITISH ISLES · North Sea · Baltic Sea · GERMANIC PEOPLES · ATLANTIC OCEAN · GAUL · Danube · Alps · Blac Sea · IBERIA · CORSICA · Rome · Constantinople · SARDINIA · Sicily · CRETE · CYPR · Atlas Mountains · AFRICA · Mediterranean Sea

Tightly packed warriors form the *testudo* formation.

Fight Like a Turtle

ROMAN FORMATIONS developed out of an earlier Greek formation called a *phalanx.* In a phalanx, soldiers stood shoulder to shoulder. Protected by their shields, soldiers could stab between their shields with long spears or pikes. The phalanx worked very well in most situations, but it was weak against cavalry (soldiers on horseback) and war elephants. The Romans therefore developed different formations for different battle needs. The *testudo,* or "turtle" formation, for example, functioned like a phalanx but included a second row of soldiers raising their shields overhead. This provided a roof of protection against arrows and javelins (short throwing spears). Roman body armor was relatively light, so the Roman soldier relied heavily on his shield, which could protect most of his body.

Roman Empire, 117 CE

maximum extent of Roman Empire

● capital city

A S I A

Caucasus Mountains

Caspian Sea

Tigris

Euphrates

Roman legionnaires were a common sight throughout the empire. Fighting with short swords and javelins, these foot soldiers (or infantry) formed the backbone of the Roman army.

DID YOU KNOW?

When leather is boiled, it can be easily molded, and it will dry hard into the molded shape. Boiled leather thickens as it cools, making it ideal for armor. As armor, it is much lighter than metal, improving a warrior's mobility. That's a primary concern if you're defending a large territory like the Roman Empire.

WAR CHEST

WEAPONS: Long spears and shorter javelins; short, double-edged swords called *gladii* (singular *gladius*)

SIEGE WEAPONS: Ballistas, onagers, battering rams, war towers

ARMOR: Helmets characterized by hinged cheek guards and decorated with horsehair crests. Body armor, called *lorica segmenta*, made of overlapping plates of metal or leather that had been boiled and shaped. Large rectangular or circular shields

FORTIFICATIONS: The type of fortification depended on the location and the material at hand. Romans used earth, stone, or wood.

LOCATION: Based in Rome and Constantinople (modern-day Istanbul), but spreading east into Asia, south across North Africa, west to Spain, and north into the British Isles

TIME PERIOD: Eighth century BCE to fifth century CE

ENEMIES: Persians, Berbers, Slavic tribes, Germanic tribes, Celtic tribes, Huns, Turks

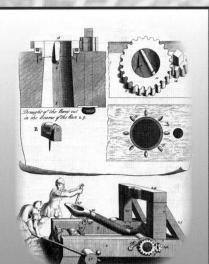

The onager was a type of catapult. It kicked like a donkey when it fired stones, so it took the name onager, which is a kind of wild donkey.

Howling, Naked Warriors

Today, only parts of Great Britain and Ireland are called "Celtic," but at their height around 200 BCE, the Celts controlled a significant portion of Europe. Their Roman and Germanic rivals knew the Celts as fierce warriors, but the Celts were also excellent craftsmen and had a vibrant tradition of storytelling that preserved the memory of many legendary heroes. The most famous of these was Cú Chulainn (pronounced "Coo Hullan"). When angered, Cú Chulainn would go into a "warp spasm," a battle fury

This Roman statue shows a defeated Celtic warrior wearing a torc. Among the Celts, torcs—metal bands around the neck—symbolized nobility and power.

where he twisted into a hideous creature of war. Celts were known for rushing naked into battle, howling like animals and hurling insults at their enemies.

The Celts favored individual bravery in battle over organized military strategy and often challenged enemies to single combat. This meant that they could be easily conquered by an army trained to work together as a military unit, such as the Roman army. Julius Caesar and his Roman army conquered the Celts in modern-day France in only seven years and later conquered Britain. Caesar wrote that Celtic charioteers were so skilled they could run quickly up the pole connecting the chariot to the horses and stand atop the yoke (a bar between the horses), then run back down into the chariot—all while driving.

DID YOU KNOW?

Among the Celts, women were warriors and leaders. Cú Chulainn is said to have been trained for war by a woman named Scáthach, while the British queen Boudica became famous for leading her people against the conquering Romans in the first century CE.

A statue of Boudica in her chariot stands in London. Boudica led a revolt against the Romans in eastern England about 60 CE.

FIVE FAMOUS CASTLES IN WALES

1. *Caerphilly:* Largest castle in Wales
2. *Caernarfon:* One of Edward I's (king of England from 1272 to 1307) "Iron Ring" castles
3. *Beaumaris:* The largest of Edward I's castles
4. *Dinas Brân:* A truly Celtic castle famous for its connections to the Holy Grail legend
5. *Cardiff:* The castle of Wales's capital city was built on earlier Roman fortresses.

King Edward I of England conquered Wales in 1284 and built an "Iron Ring" of castles to keep the Celtic Welsh in line. Caernarfon is an excellent example.

March to Certain Death

IN THE FIFTH CENTURY CE, Germanic tribes known as the Angles, Saxons, and Jutes came from northern Germany and Jutland. They settled in Britain, pushing the Celtic peoples westward and northward. In the late fifth century, the Angles invaded Bernicia in northern England. Around 600 the Battle of Catraeth (pronounced "Ca-traith") took place. The story of this battle is told in the Welsh poem *Gododdin* ("Go-do-thin"). According to the tale, 300 men of the kingdom of Gododdin marched bravely into certain death against the Angles! They fought honorably until they had all died, except for one man who escaped to tell the tale.

This fine iron blade, with a decorated bronze and gold hilt and sheath, was buried with a Celtic prince in the sixth century BCE.

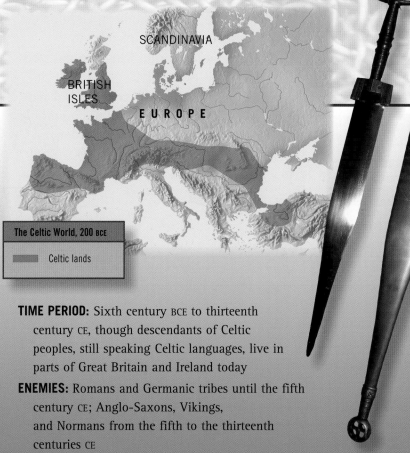

SCANDINAVIA

BRITISH ISLES

EUROPE

The Celtic World, 200 BCE

Celtic lands

WAR CHEST

WEAPONS: Primarily swords and spears. Swords were double-edged and thickened toward the center. They used war chariots as well.

ARMOR: The Celts had little body armor, though they carried shields and sometimes wore helmets. Most of the time they ran completely naked into battle!

FORTIFICATIONS: Hill forts with earthworks, some use of stone. By the thirteenth century CE, Celts were building castles of stone, though most stone castles in Celtic lands were built by non-Celtic invaders.

LOCATION: During the Middle Ages, Gaul—modern-day France—and parts of Spain, Wales, Scotland, and Ireland were the primary locations of Celtic peoples.

TIME PERIOD: Sixth century BCE to thirteenth century CE, though descendants of Celtic peoples, still speaking Celtic languages, live in parts of Great Britain and Ireland today

ENEMIES: Romans and Germanic tribes until the fifth century CE; Anglo-Saxons, Vikings, and Normans from the fifth to the thirteenth centuries CE

In the Hall of the Slain

A reproduction of a helmet found in the grave of a seventh-century CE king at the royal graveyard of Sutton Hoo in Suffolk, England.

During the migration period (about the fourth to the eighth centuries CE), Germanic peoples largely took control of the crumbling Roman Empire. There are legends about many heroes from this period—including the Asiatic conqueror Attila the Hun—but the most famous Germanic hero is Sigurd the Dragonslayer. As the greatest warrior of his day, Sigurd was so strong that he split an anvil with his sword when testing its strength and sharpness.

Fierce Warriors

The Germanic tribes were feared for their skill and ferocity in battle. Unlike Roman soldiers, Germanic warriors elected a leader in times of war and fought organized by clan or family.

Germanic warriors advanced in a wedge-shaped formation, commonly believed to be a gift from Woden,

DID YOU KNOW?

In addition to being an excellent fighter, the Germanic warrior was expected to be skilled in poetry and wise in giving advice or counsel. The Germanic god of war, Woden, was also the god of poetry and is said to have pulled out one of his own eyes as payment for a drink from the giant Mimir's well of wisdom.

called Odin in Scandinavia, the Germanic god of war. We get the word "Wednesday" from *Woden*. In this wedge-shaped formation, warriors' large round shields formed a dense wall of protection. Safely behind their shields, they could attack with spears not unlike a Greek phalanx.

Some Germanic warriors served in the Roman army before its collapse and were known for their ability to swim across rivers while fully armed. Women played an important role in war by shouting at the men during battle and inspiring them to perform great deeds. Shamed was the man who fled a fight when all the women of the tribe were watching!

WAR CHEST

WEAPONS: Light spears, throwing javelins, axes; swords made from strips of iron welded together

ARMOR: Chain mail, leather, or a mix. Sometimes no armor was worn. Iron or leather helmets and large, round, colorfully painted shields

FORTIFICATIONS: Earthworks and wooden stockades. Battles were fought in the open so fortifications were generally unnecessary.

LOCATION: The region around the Black Sea, Scandinavia, and modern Germany, spreading as far west as Spain

TIME PERIOD: As early as the eighth century BCE to the eighth century CE

MAIN ENEMIES: The Huns, the Romans, and the Celts

A golden ornament, worn at the shoulder, from Sutton Hoo. Germanic kings were expected to distribute gold, jewelry, and other spoils of war among their warriors.

Warrior's Paradise

This rune stone may show a valkyrie (divine female warriors of Scandinavia) and Odin on his eight-legged horse welcoming a warrior to Valhalla.

THE GERMANIC PEOPLES became famous for their desire to die gloriously in battle for their king. Glory was seen as a kind of immortality. The Germanic heaven was called Valhalla, or "The Hall of the Slain," and only the best warriors could get in. Here, heroes would fight each other every day, hacking one another to pieces. But every evening they would become whole again to feast on boar meat and drink mead, a wine made from honey.

This rune stone shows the hero Sigurd, at the very top, slaying the dragon Fafnir, whose body wraps around the stone's edge and contains the actual runes.

SCANDINAVIA

North Sea

BRITISH ISLES

ATLANTIC OCEAN

ASIA

Black Sea

Mediterranean Sea

AFRICA

Germanic Territory, c. 100–800 CE	
▬	Germanic settlement region

SECRET LETTERS

THE GERMANIC PEOPLES used their own alphabet, known as the runic alphabet, or *futhark*. It consisted of 24 angular shapes that could easily be carved in stone and other hard objects. The word *rune* means "secret" or "mystery." Runes were sometimes used for magical purposes, but they were also carved on huge stones to commemorate fallen warriors.

Fury of the North

The term "Viking" applies to seafaring warriors from Scandinavia. Vikings used their amazing longships to raid, plunder, and trade from the eighth through the twelfth centuries CE—a period now known as the Viking Age. Most people were terrified of the Vikings. They seemed to appear from nowhere, sack (raid and destroy) a city, and disappear before anyone could chase them. Vikings had the best ship-making technology of their day.

A Viking sword. Vikings used swords, axes, and spears, all made from iron.

HANGING OUT WITH VIKINGS

IN 845 CE, Vikings sailed up the Seine River to Paris. Along the way, they defeated a Frankish army and hanged 111 prisoners on trees along the riverbank. Another Frankish army on the opposite shore was so horrified that they fled in terror! This left the Vikings free to sail farther upstream to Paris.

DID YOU KNOW?

The phrase "to go berserk," meaning to become wild and crazy, comes from Old Norse, the Viking language. Viking berserkers worked themselves into a battle fury, howling like wolves and biting their shields. While enraged, berserkers supposedly could not be cut by swords or spears and had the strength of many men.

Up the River

The largest Viking ships could probably hold more than 100 warriors. Despite their size, these ships could sail in less than three feet of water, allowing Vikings to sail far upstream in shallow rivers. Vikings used Europe's rivers for both raiding and trading. Viking trade extended so far eastward that statues of Buddha, all the way from eastern Asia, have been found in Viking graves!

Shields and Shield Maidens

Viking Age women were strong figures, often telling men when and whom to fight. In the legends, women sometimes decided to live as warriors and became "shield maidens." The most famous of these is Brynhild in the tale of Sigurd the Dragonslayer.

Fighting was a major activity for most Viking men. Since warriors were more heavily armed up top, and Viking shields didn't reach far below the knee, injuries to the legs were common. Sometimes a warrior suffered the misfortune of having both legs cut out from under him in a single blow. At least he wouldn't suffer the disgrace of running away!

This popular Viking Age image shows what may be Odin (or Woden) on the left and a berserker on the right. Half-man, half-wolf, this figure may also be an *ulfhednar*, or wolf-shirt warrior.

A remarkable piece of Viking carving decorated the Oseberg ship, which was buried in the ninth century CE as part of a noble funeral

GREENLAND

ARCTIC OCEAN

HELLULAND

ICELAND
★ Reykjavik

★ Trondheim

NORWAY SWEDEN
★ Uppsala
★ Birka

North
Sea

NORTH
AMERICA

★ Trelleborg

IRELAND   ENGLAND   DENMARK   POLAND   KIEVAN RUS
Dublin ★   ★ York

VINLAND   ★ L'Anse aux Meadows
• London   HOLY
ROMAN   HUNGARY   • Kiev   Don
• Paris   EMPIRE

St. Lawrence   NEWFOUNDLAND

Volga

Dnieper

FRANCE

Caspian
Sea

ATLANTIC OCEAN

Black Sea

UMAYYAD SPAIN   Rome •   • Constantinople

BYZANTINE EMPIRE

• Seville   Mediterranean Sea

Tigris
Euphrates

Viking World, c. 1000 ᴄᴇ

— Viking routes
▬ Viking settlement
• city
★ Viking town

• Cairo

Nile

A F R I C A

The Oseberg ship

Norse in North America

SHORTLY BEFORE THE YEAR 1000 ᴄᴇ, Icelandic Vikings discovered
Greenland and a land they called Vinland. The voyages of Icelanders
to Vinland were believed to be fictional until archaeologists found the
ruins of a Norse (Scandinavian) settlement in L'Anse aux Meadows in
Newfoundland, Canada. So Vikings made it all the way to North America,
nearly 500 years before Christopher Columbus! The Norse called
American Indians *Skrælingjar* or "Shriekers."

The Steed and the Rider

Early in the Middle Ages, warriors usually rode their horses to the battleground, dismounted, and fought on foot. Starting around the eighth century CE, new technology helped change that. Stirrups and better saddles allowed warriors to sit more firmly on horseback, or even stand in the stirrups. Sitting securely in the saddle, a warrior could drive a lance, the mounted knight's primary weapon, into an opponent at a full gallop. With all the weight of the horse and rider behind the blow, there could be more than 1,000 pounds behind every thrust! No wonder this new form of mounted knight quickly dominated the battleground.

THE NASTIEST WEAPONS OF THE HIGH MIDDLE AGES

1. *Boiling oil:* poured from castle walls onto attacking knights
2. *Caltrops:* barbs placed on the ground for horses to step on
3. *Horse sword:* a long, wavy sword for cutting horses
4. *Crossbow:* Crossbows could pierce even plate armor.
5. *Flail:* a spiked ball on a chain

A flail

WAR CHEST

WEAPONS: Long spears or lances, swords, maces, flails

ARMOR: Full suits of chain mail or plate armor, great helms or helmets with face guards. Large, kite-shaped shields

FORTIFICATIONS: Stone castles

LOCATION: All across Europe and into Asia

TIME PERIOD: Eighth through sixteenth centuries CE

MAIN ENEMIES: Other knights, Huns, and various Islamic empires

The open-faced helmets of the early Middle Ages gave way to the great helm, which offered plenty of protection but limited visibility.

Medieval Tank

As knights became more comfortable on horseback, they did not need to move around as much on foot. They could therefore wear heavier armor. Over time, individual plates of steel were added to suits of chain mail to protect vulnerable parts of the rider's body. Eventually, so many plates were added that they covered the entire knight. Plate armor covered knights so completely that warriors needed heraldry—signs painted on armor and clothing—to tell friends from foes. A full suit of plate armor could weigh more then 60 pounds. Nonetheless, trained knights were capable of leaping onto their horses in full armor, chasing enemies on foot, and climbing ladders. Even the horses wore armor!

The Middle Ages

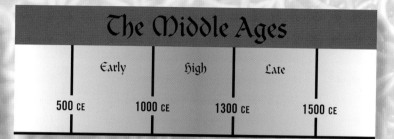

	Early	High	Late	
500 CE		1000 CE	1300 CE	1500 CE

Jousting was a spectator sport, widely popular in the High Middle Ages. In a joust, two mounted knights charged at each other, each trying to knock the other off his horse with a lance.

A classic image of the mounted knight, whose battered shield shows evidence of his profession

From Farm to Battlefield

A SINGLE SUIT OF CHAIN MAIL took tens of thousands of links and hundreds of hours of work to make. For these reasons, armor was very expensive. Only wealthy warriors could afford good armor. Strange though it sounds, advancements in farming technology helped make the rise of mounted warriors possible. Technology allowed fewer people to produce more food. Selling the extra food created more wealth in Europe. This allowed knights to afford the horses, war gear, and servants they needed.

Chain mail

Vikings of France

The name "Norman" comes from "North Man" because the Normans originally came from the North—they were Vikings who had settled in northern France. Like their Viking predecessors, the Normans were fierce warriors. They conquered large portions of France and England and played an important role in the Crusades. They even established kingdoms in Sicily and southern Italy.

Tapestry of Conquest

The Normans are best known for their conquest of England, when William the Conqueror defeated the English King Harold at the Battle of Hastings in 1066 CE. The Bayeux Tapestry shows the story of this battle. The tapestry is a 230-foot-long piece of cloth embroidered (by hand!) with scenes of the conquest. William himself was said to be so strong that no one else could draw his bow, and he could shoot it while riding horseback.

A Norman Castle

Norman castles usually consisted of a central tower—known as the "keep"—built on top of a high, steep mound of earth. The mound was surrounded by a moat (a ditch often filled with water), and some distance away from the moat stood the outer walls. This type of castle was quick to build, difficult to capture, and easy to defend. If their supplies lasted, just a handful of brave warriors could hold the keep for days or even weeks against a large army. Because only a few soldiers were needed at each castle, the Normans could easily control large territories.

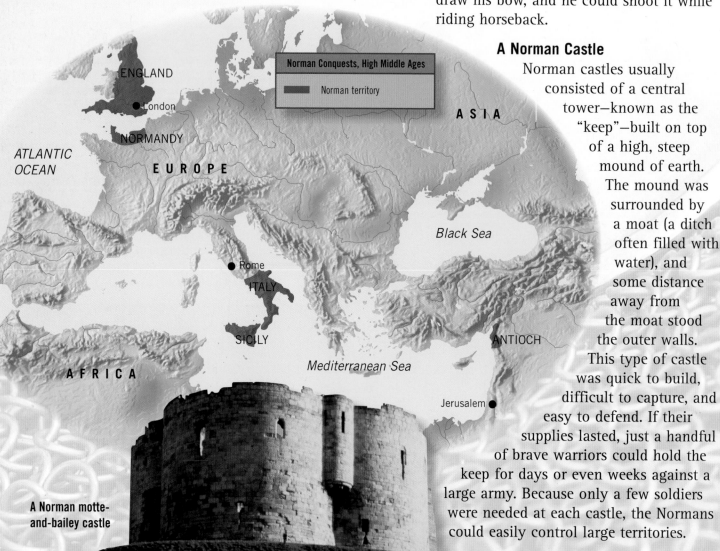

Norman Conquests, High Middle Ages

Norman territory

ENGLAND
London
NORMANDY
ATLANTIC OCEAN
EUROPE
ASIA
Black Sea
Rome
ITALY
SICILY
ANTIOCH
Mediterranean Sea
AFRICA
Jerusalem

A Norman motte-and-bailey castle

THE BATTLE OF HASTINGS

KING HAROLD OF ENGLAND met William of Normandy at the Battle of Hastings on October 14, 1066. King Harold had recently defeated a Danish army in the north of England at the Battle of Stamford Bridge. He and his troops had to rush south to meet William's invading force. The English, exhausted from the march, fought on top of Senlac Hill, north of Hastings, and held their defensive shield wall tightly. William faked a retreat and the English broke the shield wall to chase the enemy. The Normans then turned and routed the disorganized English forces (to rout means to completely defeat the enemy or to make them flee). Harold died from an arrow shot into his eye.

A scene from the Bayeux Tapestry, showing King Harold on the far right with an arrow in his eye

A Norman knight. Normans wore distinctive cone-shaped helmets, with a bar in front to protect the nose.

WAR CHEST

WEAPONS: Long spears or lances, javelins, swords, battle-axes, bows and arrows

ARMOR: Full suits of chain mail, covering even the legs; conical helmets with nose-guards; and large kite-shaped shields

FORTIFICATIONS: Stone castles with a central keep and moat called "motte-and-bailey" castles, as well as larger stone castles

LOCATION: Northern France, England, Sicily, southern Italy, and the Holy Land

TIME PERIOD: Tenth through thirteenth centuries CE

MAIN ENEMIES: Anglo-Saxons, Saracens, Byzantines, other Normans

Knights of the Cross

For nearly three centuries, Christian Europe waged war on Muslims—often called Saracens in medieval times—living in Western Asia, North Africa, and even Spain. A series of leaders, including kings and popes, sought to capture lands that they viewed as Christian (and therefore rightfully theirs). Central to these campaigns was Jerusalem, a holy city in Christianity, Islam, and Judaism. In time, these expeditions became known as the Crusades (from the Latin word for "cross") because of the crosses Christian warriors wore on their armor.

The First Crusade began in 1095. Most early crusaders were Frankish (from France) or Norman, but later on, crusaders came from all over Europe. Crusaders on horseback and on foot traveled over land and sea to get to the so-called Holy Land. These voyages were long and difficult, and many died along the way. Disease and hunger were enemies as fierce as the Saracens!

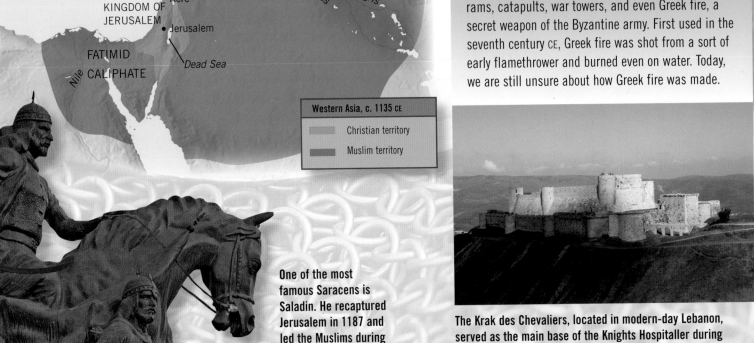

Map labels

BYZANTINE EMPIRE
SULTANATE OF RÛM
Konya
ARMENIAN KINGDOM OF CILICIA
EDESSA
Tarsus
Edessa
Harran
BYZANTINE EMPIRE
ANTIOCH
Aleppo
Antioch
Cyprus
GREAT SELJUK EMPIRE
TRIPOLI
Tripoli
Mediterranean Sea
Euphrates
Tigris
Damascus
Acre
KINGDOM OF JERUSALEM
Jerusalem
FATIMID CALIPHATE
Nile
Dead Sea

Western Asia, c. 1135 CE

Christian territory
Muslim territory

One of the most famous Saracens is Saladin. He recaptured Jerusalem in 1187 and led the Muslims during the Third Crusade.

The Secret Flame

CRUSADERS USED the armor and weapons of their day: chain mail, double-edged broadswords, spears, and kite-shaped shields. In addition, Crusaders used a number of siege weapons, including battering rams, catapults, war towers, and even Greek fire, a secret weapon of the Byzantine army. First used in the seventh century CE, Greek fire was shot from a sort of early flamethrower and burned even on water. Today, we are still unsure about how Greek fire was made.

The Krak des Chevaliers, located in modern-day Lebanon, served as the main base of the Knights Hospitaller during the Crusades.

During the Crusades, Christian warriors created religious military orders such as the Knights Templar, the Hospitallers, and the Teutonic Knights. The Templars famously wore white surcoats with red crosses.

THE NINE CRUSADES

1. *1096–1099:* Crusaders capture Jerusalem.
2. *1147–1148:* Edessa lost to Muslims
3. *1187–1192:* Saladin recaptures Jerusalem.
4. *1202–1204:* Crusaders sack Constantinople.
5. *1217–1221:* Austrian and Hungarian forces try to recapture Jerusalem (and fail).
6. *1228–1229:* Friedrich II of Germany negotiates partial control of Jerusalem.
7. *1248–1254:* A failed attempt to avenge defeated Crusaders in Gaza
8. *1270:* A failed attempt to help Crusaders in Syria
9. *1271–1272:* After Louis IX of France fails to capture the Holy Land, Edward I of England tries unsuccessfully to carry out the same mission.

The First Crusade, 1096–1099 CE

- routes of the First Crusade
- Christian territory
- Muslim territory
- shared Christian and Muslim regions
- ✕ major battles

ATLANTIC OCEAN

North Sea

London
Utrecht
Boulogne
Gand
Bouillon
Paris
Blois
Vienna
Bordeaux
Toulouse
Marseille
Rome
Naples
Durrës
Taranto
Constantinople
Black Sea
Caspian Sea
Palermo
Mediterranean Sea
Jerusalem
Ascalon

Warriors of Africa

Second only to Asia in size among the continents, Africa is so big you could fit all of Europe, the United States, and Australia into it and still have room left over! Africa has been home to numerous peoples, cultures, and, of course, warriors. In general, we know surprisingly little about the history of many African peoples. There are relatively few written documents, making it hard to learn about cultures of the past, and archaeologists still need to dig up many places important to African history.

One thing is certain, however: Africa is a land of both mystery and might. From the famous Egyptians of the ancient Nile valley to the Zulu spearmen of South Africa, this continent has produced great kingdoms, powerful tribes, and fierce fighters. In this section, we'll look at warriors from across the African continent. We'll explore great civilizations that have long since vanished and tribes that even today feast on the meat of their herds.

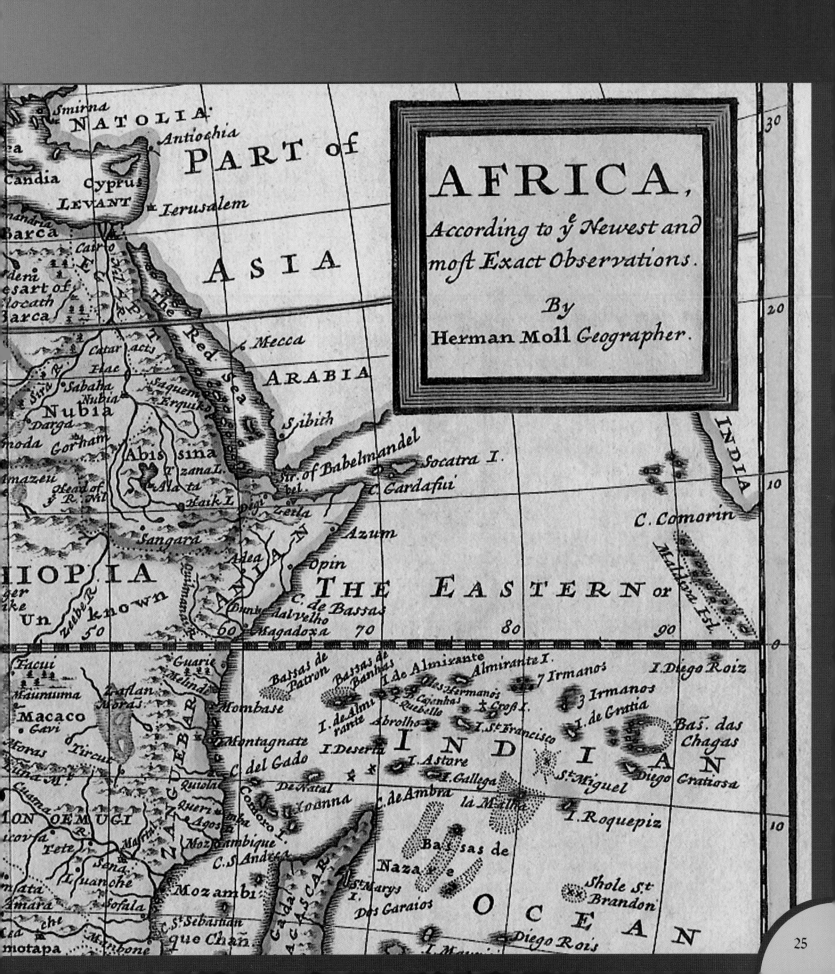

AFRICA,

According to y^e Newest and most Exact Observations.

By

Herman Moll Geographer.

PART of ASIA

NATOLIA

Smirna
Antiochia
Candia   Cyprus
LEVANT   Ierusalem
andria
Barca
Cairo
dera
esart of
locath
Barca
Catar acts
Flae
Sib   Sabatha   Nubia
Nubia   Erquko
Darga
moda   Gorham
Abissina
mazeu   Tzana L.
Head of   Ala ta
ye R. nil   Haik L.   Digi
Sangara   Zetla
HIOPIA   Un known   Adea
iger   Opin
rike   Zaebe R.   50   Dinne   dal velho   Magadoxa
C. de Bassas

The Red Sea

ARABIA

Mecca

S.ibith

Str. of Babelmandel
bel   C. Gardafui   Socatra I.

Azum

THE   EASTERN or

60   70   80   90   0

ARABIA

INDIA

C. Comorin

Maldiva Isl.

Facui
Maunuma
Macaco
Gavi
Moras
Tircut   Aflan   Moras
Cuama   Quiola
ana M.   Mafia
ION OEMUGI   Queri
icowfa   Agosa   inka
Tete   Mafia
Sena   Lsuanche
sata   Amara   Mozambi
Marbone
motapa   St. Sebastian
que Chan
Sofala

Guarie
Melind
Mombase
Montagnate
del Gado
C. del Gado
Quiola
De Natal
Ioanna
Comoro I.

Bassas de
Patron
Bassas de
Banhas   I. de Almirante   Almirante I.
I. de Almi   Iles Hermanos   7 Irmanos
rante   P. Cajenhas   Crofs I.
Abrolho   I. Quebello   I. St Francisto
I. Deseria   I.   N   I. de Gratia
I. Astore
I. Gallega   St Miguel
C. de Ambra   la Malha
Naza   Roquepiz
Bassas de
St Marys   Naza
I.
Des Garaios   OCEAN   Shole St.
Diego Rois   Brandon
I. Mauri

I. Diego Roiz
3 Irmanos
Bas. das
Chagas
Diego
Gratiosa

The Might of the Nile

The kingdom of the ancient Egyptians was one of the oldest civilizations in the world, and we marvel even now at its feats of art and architecture, many of which were preserved in the dry desert sands. As the Egyptians' technology developed, their military improved, and their empire grew into one of the world's greatest civilizations.

Chariot Archers

Despite developing the greatest technology of their day, Egyptians did not know about iron, so they made most of their tools and weapons from copper or bronze. After the Hyksos conquered Egypt in the seventeenth century BCE, Egyptians began using chariots and a different kind of bow, more powerful than what they had used before. The prized weapon of the elite Egyptian warrior became the bow and arrow. Chariots were manned with two warriors: one to steer the horses and one to shoot at the enemy. This arrangement allowed the Egyptian archer to shoot continuously. Pharaoh Amenhotep II (1427–1400 BCE) was famous for his skill in archery. Nobody else could draw his bow, and the pharaoh could pierce four targets while riding by in his chariot. The targets were made of copper and were as thick as a person's palm.

More than 5,000 years old, the Narmer Palette shows what may be Egypt's first pharaoh, Narmer, subduing his enemies. With some of the earliest hieroglyphs (Egyptian writing) ever found, the palette may show Narmer uniting Egypt.

Egypt is known for its great pyramids of Giza and their enormous guardian, the Sphinx.

A Warrior's Life

Egyptian warriors trained for fighting by practicing a number of sports, such as target archery, swimming, running, jumping, rowing, wrestling, boxing, and stick fighting. When not at war, Egyptian warriors would develop their strength and bravery by hunting some of the large beasts of Africa, such as lions, elephants, and even hippopotamuses!

Magic and Medicine

GREAT TRADITIONS OF WAR often come with great traditions of healing. The Egyptians were known for their health and medical knowledge. Many medical documents have survived, showing medicine to be inseparable from Egyptian magic. Remedies often included bizarre substances, such as the blood and urine of bats!

A scarab, a popular amulet in ancient Egypt

An Egyptian chariot archer

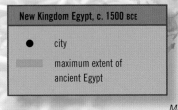

New Kingdom Egypt, c. 1500 BCE

- ● city
- maximum extent of ancient Egypt

HITTITES

Cyprus

Mediterranean Sea

• Ugarit

• Byblos
• Tyre

• Jerusalem

• Piramesse

• Memphis

Sahara Desert

•Akhetaten

• Abydos
• Thebes

• Elephantine

Nile

Red Sea

NUBIA

WAR CHEST

WEAPONS: Bronze swords, scimitars, daggers, and axes; javelins; composite bows and arrows; slings and stones

ARMOR: Mostly no body armor, but occasionally leather or scale armor. Shields of wood and leather

FORTIFICATIONS: Forts of mud brick and occasionally stone. Forts were placed on the Nile or on hills overlooking the river.

LOCATION: Nile River valley in Egypt

TIME PERIOD: Fourth millennium BCE to the fourth century BCE

MAIN ENEMIES: Hyksos, Hittites, Nubians, Bedouins

A bronze Egyptian scimitar

Desert Kings of Islam

The Umayyad Empire, or Caliphate, was one of the great civilizations of the world, and certainly was one of the most important during the Middle Ages. The Umayyad Empire is known as a caliphate because its leader was called a caliph. At the height of its glory in the eighth century CE, the Umayyad Caliphate was the largest empire ever, covering a landmass larger than the European continent. Its advanced technology and sophisticated society could hardly be outdone in its day.

DID YOU KNOW?

The Umayyads rose to great power by fierce and often ruthless leadership. One Arab governor, al-Hajjâj ibn Yûsuf, cut off the heads of as many as 120,000 people to enforce loyalty to the caliph!

Spread of the Caliphate

The Umayyad Caliphate grew quickly under superb military leadership. From its base on the Arabian peninsula it even conquered Spain. Umayyads set up an Islamic kingdom there called Al-Andalus.

The Dome of the Rock in Jerusalem is the oldest intact Islamic building. It was completed in 691 and during the Crusades actually served as a base for the Templars of Europe.

WAR CHEST

WEAPONS: Long spears and javelins; straight, double-edged and curved, single-edged swords or scimitars; maces and axes; composite bows

SIEGE WEAPONS: Ballistas, mangonels, battering rams

ARMOR: Chain mail or scale armor with large shields; helmets with chain mail draped from the back and often with some form of face protection

FORTIFICATIONS: Large castles and fortifications of stone and brick

LOCATION: Based in Damascus, but stretching as far west as Portugal and as far east as northern India

TIME PERIOD: Seventh to eighth centuries CE

MAIN ENEMIES: North African Berbers, the Byzantine Empire, the Persians, and various European kingdoms

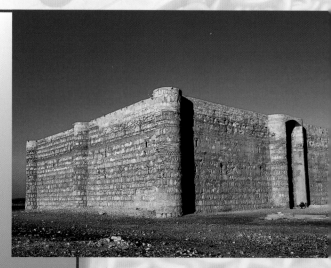

The Umayyad fortress Qasr Kharana stands in the western Syrian Desert.

The Arabs in Spain were called "Moors" and were feared and respected for their courage in battle. The Umayyads nearly made it into France, too, but the Frankish king, Charles Martel, halted them in 732 at the Battle of Poitiers.

The Umayyads often fought with the Byzantines, but never managed to capture the Byzantine capital of Constantinople. In 715, Sulayman ibn Abd al-Malik became caliph and launched a massive attack on Constantinople, by both land and sea, with tens of thousands of soldiers. But the strong city walls held off the land attack while deadly Greek fire stopped the Arab warships at sea. Like the Battle of Poitiers, this crucial Byzantine victory stopped the Muslim caliphate from advancing into Europe.

Age of Caliphs, c. 750 CE	
▭	maximum extent of Umayyad Empire
●	city
✕	major battle

The Battle of Poitiers halted the Umayyad advance from Spain into western Europe, a major victory for Christian Europe. Spain would remain under Islamic control until the fifteenth century.

CONQUEST OF IBERIA

IN 711 CE, Tariq ibn Ziyad captured the Visigothic kingdom of the Iberian Peninsula, home of present-day Spain and Portugal. Tariq came by sea from Morocco with a massive army. According to legend, he burned his army's ships after crossing the Strait of Gibraltar. That way there could be no retreat: either they would conquer, or they would die. Fortunately for them, they conquered and established Al-Andalus, which quickly became a center of scholarship and learning for the rest of Europe.

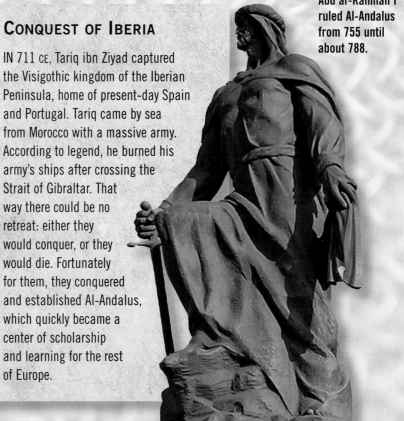

Abd ar-Rahman I ruled Al-Andalus from 755 until about 788.

Mysteries in Stone

The African nation of Zimbabwe takes its name from the ancient city of Great Zimbabwe. Today, Great Zimbabwe lies in ruins, consisting of large stone dwellings and walls. Though scholars are not entirely certain, the word *Zimbabwe* could mean "house of stone," referring to these stone buildings. Its builders constructed the city gradually, from the eleventh to fifteenth centuries CE, until Great Zimbabwe covered nearly 200 square miles.

At its height, as many as 18,000 people called Great Zimbabwe home. Archaeological excavations (dig sites) in Great Zimbabwe have revealed objects from as far away as China. Great Zimbabwe must have been an important center for trade, but its inhabitants abandoned the city by the middle of the sixteenth century, leaving only a mystery behind them. No one knows for sure who built Great Zimbabwe, or why this once flourishing civilization disappeared.

The people of Great Zimbabwe probably relied heavily on spears such as this one.

WAR CHEST

WEAPONS: Iron spears, bows and arrows

ARMOR: Probably no body armor, but likely shields of wood and leather

FORTIFICATIONS: Unknown

LOCATION: Plateau south of the Zambezi River in modern-day Zimbabwe

TIME PERIOD: Eleventh to sixteenth centuries CE

MAIN ENEMIES: Unknown. Later Shona peoples fought among themselves and against Portuguese invaders.

WAR IN ZIMBABWE

WE DON'T KNOW much about how the people of Great Zimbabwe fought their enemies—or even who those enemies were. Nonetheless, iron spear- and arrowheads found in the ruins indicate that warfare was not unlike that found among nearby tribes, and warriors likely used wooden and leather shields.

Researchers are fairly certain that the stone walls of Great Zimbabwe, which reach as high as 36 feet, were not meant for defense. Instead, the walls made up the lavish palaces of the chieftain and royal house. Most of the common folk lived in huts made of a material called *daga*, a clay filled with granite. When baked in the sun, *daga* hardened like cement. The city must have taken tremendous organization to build. From this we can guess that the people of Great Zimbabwe organized their military with similar sophistication.

This stone tower in Great Zimbabwe was built from stones stacked without mortar, like the rest of the ruins. It is more than 30 feet tall.

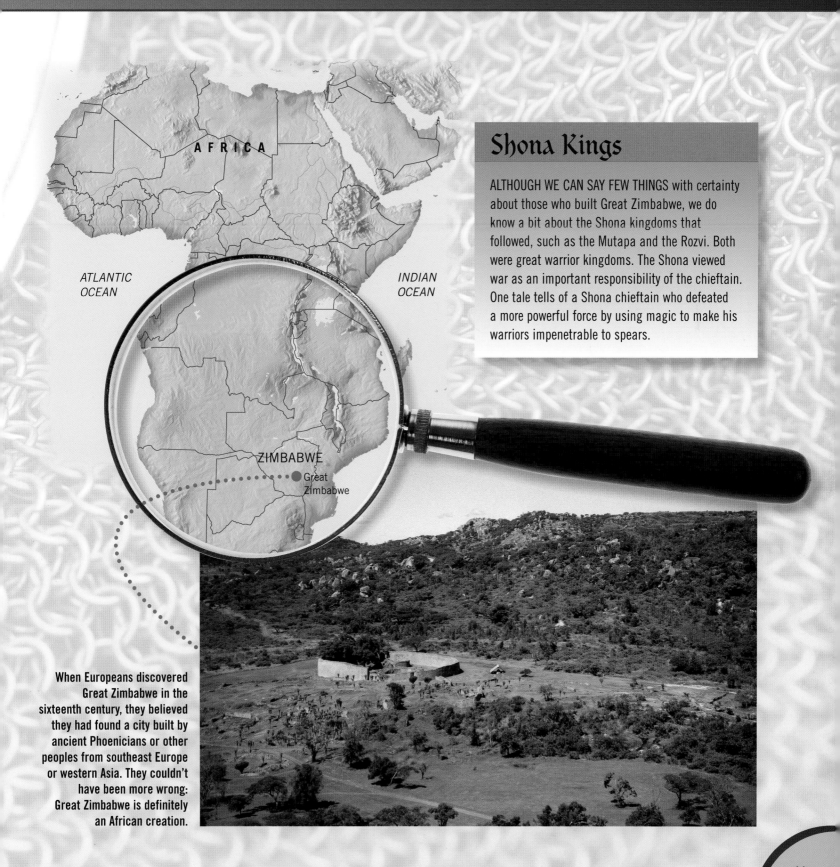

AFRICA

ATLANTIC OCEAN

INDIAN OCEAN

ZIMBABWE

● Great Zimbabwe

Shona Kings

ALTHOUGH WE CAN SAY FEW THINGS with certainty about those who built Great Zimbabwe, we do know a bit about the Shona kingdoms that followed, such as the Mutapa and the Rozvi. Both were great warrior kingdoms. The Shona viewed war as an important responsibility of the chieftain. One tale tells of a Shona chieftain who defeated a more powerful force by using magic to make his warriors impenetrable to spears.

When Europeans discovered Great Zimbabwe in the sixteenth century, they believed they had found a city built by ancient Phoenicians or other peoples from southeast Europe or western Asia. They couldn't have been more wrong: Great Zimbabwe is definitely an African creation.

Spears Through the Heart

The Zulu live in the Natal region of South Africa. They have a rich history as one of the dominant military powers of southern Africa in the last few centuries. Zulu warriors were especially feared and respected by British and Dutch invaders in the nineteenth century.

The Zulu rose to power in the early nineteenth century under a skilled warrior-king named Shaka. As a teenager, Shaka began to show his prowess as a warrior, practicing stick fighting regularly and hunting wild animals. Shaka quickly rose through the ranks in the army because of his bravery and leadership.

Shaka was a ruthless leader and was known for slaughtering his enemies, even after they had surrendered. He even killed women, children, and the elderly. Through his ferocity, he united many smaller tribes under the power of the Zulu nation. His descendants fought against the British, who learned to fear the Zulu in the Anglo-Zulu War of 1879. Although the Zulu were eventually defeated, their skill and bravery in many bloody battles left a permanent impression in the hearts of the British military.

A Zulu warrior

DEMOCRATIC REPUBLIC OF THE CONGO

ATLANTIC OCEAN

ANGOLA

ZAMBIA

NAMIBIA

BOTSWANA

ZIMBABWE

MOZAMBIQUE

SOUTH AFRICA

SWAZILAND

LESOTHO

TANZANIA

MADAGASCAR

INDIAN OCEAN

Southern Africa

maximum extent of the Zulu nation

British forces suffered a major defeat on January 22, 1879, at the Battle of Isandlwana during the Anglo-Zulu War. Of some 1,500 British fighters, fewer than 100 survived.

WAR CHEST

WEAPONS: Iron spears called *assegai*; throwing javelins, and clubs called knobkerries

ARMOR: No body armor. Shields of wood and cowhide pointed at either end. They varied in size from under two feet to full body length.

FORTIFICATIONS: None, but they used the natural terrain to their advantage.

LOCATION: South Africa

TIME PERIOD: Late eighteenth century CE to the present day

MAIN ENEMIES: Other Nguni tribes such as the Ndwandwe, British and Dutch colonists

A Zulu spear

Keep Your Enemies Closer

DID YOU KNOW?

Shaka made his army go barefoot, discarding their traditional sandals, because this meant that they could move much faster. Their mobility allowed them to outmaneuver and chase down opponents.

SHAKA DEVELOPED A NEW METHOD of fighting that quickly outstripped the abilities of neighboring tribes. Previously, the standard method of fighting was to throw spears at each other from a distance. Shaka developed a shorter spear for stabbing. He would use his own shield to hook his opponent's shield and expose the enemy's chest. Then he would use his short spear to stab the enemy's heart. Shaka demonstrated this method of fighting in single combat before two large armies. Striding out before his own army, he avoided the spear throws of his opponent, ran up, hooked the shield, and stabbed so forcefully that his spear ripped all the way through his enemy's chest. Not stopping there, Shaka leapt over the dead body and charged alone at the opposing army.

The great Zulu king, Shaka

Warriors of the Herd

The Masai live in eastern Africa, mainly in Kenya and Tanzania. They are so devoted to their cattle that their warriors exist only to protect their herds and to acquire more animals by raiding. They believe that all cattle in the world belong to them, so they see their raids as merely reclaiming what is already theirs.

Warrior Initiation

Only males become warriors, or *moran*, and they do so in large groups according to age. When the members of an age group become warriors, they go to live in a special village called a *manyatta*. Once they are fully warriors, they protect the herds from thieves and deadly animals, such as leopards and lions.

Tools of the Warrior

As well as protecting their own cattle, Masai warriors are also responsible for getting more cattle by raiding other villages. Warriors use swords, spears, and throwing clubs. The Masai spear is unique. It is almost six feet in length, has a pointed steel butt, a wooden handle, and a steel blade more than two feet long. Warriors train for years to throw it with astonishing force and accuracy. They usually practice by throwing the spear backward so as not to damage the blade.

Young warriors often retreat to special camps to rest and recover. These are called *olpuls* or *orpuls*. Here, they gain strength by eating lots of meat and drinking a special herbal brew. This can cause the *moran* to shake violently and foam at the mouth. At these camps, warriors train and learn about battle, as well as plan raids on nearby herds.

DID YOU KNOW?

The Masai rely on the moon to measure the passage of time. They only perform certain actions during specific phases of the moon or when the moon appears a certain color. For instance, warriors only attack on a raid when the moon looks red.

A young *moran*

Drinking Blood

IN ADDITION TO EATING the meat and dairy products of their cattle, the Masai drink the fresh blood of their livestock. They have developed a special method of piercing the jugular vein to drain blood without killing the animal. Sometimes they drink the blood fresh and pure, but during the warriors' initiation ceremony they mix it with an alcoholic beverage made from honey and ginger.

The Masai are seminomadic, which means they travel with their herds instead of living in one place year-round.

WAR CHEST

WEAPONS: Steel swords, spears, clubs

ARMOR: Mostly no body armor, but shields of wood and leather

FORTIFICATIONS: Enclosures of thorn bush fences protect the village and cattle

LOCATION: Great Rift Valley in East Africa

TIME PERIOD: Fifteenth century CE to the present day

MAIN ENEMIES: Other tribes, cattle owners, thieves, leopards, and lions

A Masai shield

The Masai are known as spirited singers and dancers. Here, Masai warriors join in a dance characterized by high jumps.

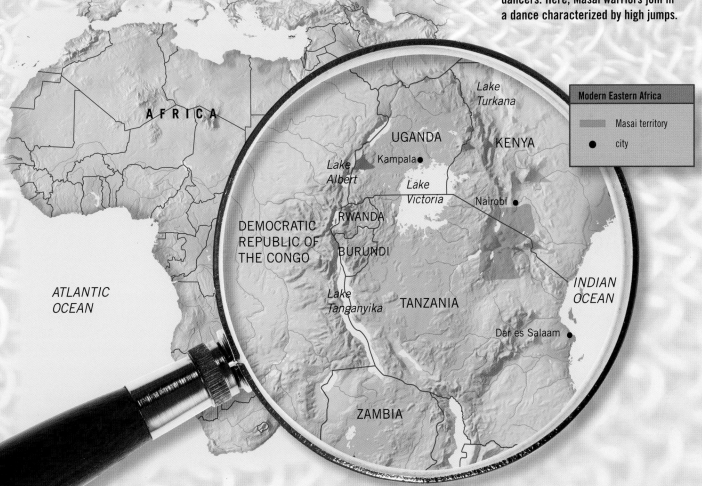

AFRICA

ATLANTIC OCEAN

Lake Turkana

UGANDA

Lake Albert

Kampala •

KENYA

Lake Victoria

Nairobi •

DEMOCRATIC REPUBLIC OF THE CONGO

RWANDA

BURUNDI

Lake Tanganyika

TANZANIA

INDIAN OCEAN

Dar es Salaam •

ZAMBIA

Modern Eastern Africa

Masai territory

• city

In the Forest of Gold

The Ashanti live in the West African region known as the Gold Coast. As the name suggests, this region is very rich in gold. It is also covered with incredibly dense forest. Like the Zulu, the Ashanti found strength in organization and unification. They incorporated conquered tribes into their own until they had grown into a huge power capable of fielding massive armies. By the early eighteenth century, the Ashanti dominated western Africa.

As a result of European influence, Ashanti warriors started using guns in warfare.

Trappings of Power

The chieftain Osei Tutu united the Ashanti in about 1700. He created symbols to help the Ashanti think of themselves as one people, much like flags of countries today. Osei used a golden stool and a royal crown made of elephant skin. His successor, Opuku Ware, was perhaps the most powerful Ashanti king. He used a sword called Mpomponsa, and everyone swore allegiance to the king on this sword.

An Ashanti *caboceer*, or slave raider, charged by the chief to acquire slaves to sell to European traders

GOLDEN STOOL

THE NATIONAL SYMBOL of the Ashanti is the Golden Stool. Stools had been symbols of leadership among chieftains, but when Osei Tutu unified the Ashanti, his head adviser created a wooden stool adorned with gold. Osei Tutu claimed that the stool had floated down from heaven and had been placed on his lap. It supposedly held the spirit of the Ashanti. This gave the Ashanti a symbol to unite under as a nation; they were no longer just a collection of tribes. Even today, the stool receives the entire nation's protection, and is only taken out on special ceremonial occasions.

The Ashanti court of King Opoku Ware II (1919–1999), ready to celebrate the monarchy's 300th anniversary in 1995. The king is seated center beside the Golden Stool.

Brave and Chivalrous

The Ashanti greatly valued bravery and enforced it severely on the battlefield. Cowards were put to death. It was not uncommon for Ashanti warriors to stride out into danger ahead of the army to cut off the head of an enemy. The severed heads became trophies of war.

Europeans praised the Ashanti not only as great fighters, but also as chivalrous warriors. They always heeded flags of surrender and never fired when offered a truce. Despite their chivalry in battle, the Ashanti were also key players in the slave trade, selling captives to European slave traders from the sixteenth to nineteenth centuries.

Ashanti Empire

☐ Ashanti Empire

MAURITANIA · MALI · NIGER · SENEGAL · Niger · GUINEA BISSAU · GUINEA · BURKINA FASO · SIERRA LEONE · COTE D'IVOIRE · GHANA · BENIN · TOGO · NIGERIA · LIBERIA · CAMEROON · ATLANTIC OCEAN

The brutal Atlantic slave trade removed millions of Africans to the Americas and other European holdings. Some African peoples, like the Ashanti, would capture members of enemy nations and sell them to European slavers.

DID YOU KNOW?

The organization of the Ashanti army supposedly came from observing ants, one of the only creatures other than humans to make war. Like ants, Ashanti warriors moved in columns that came together to meet the enemy. The army was divided into scouts, an advance guard, the main body, the king's bodyguard, the rearguard, and left and right wings. Moving in columns was the most efficient way to get through the dense forests of western Africa.

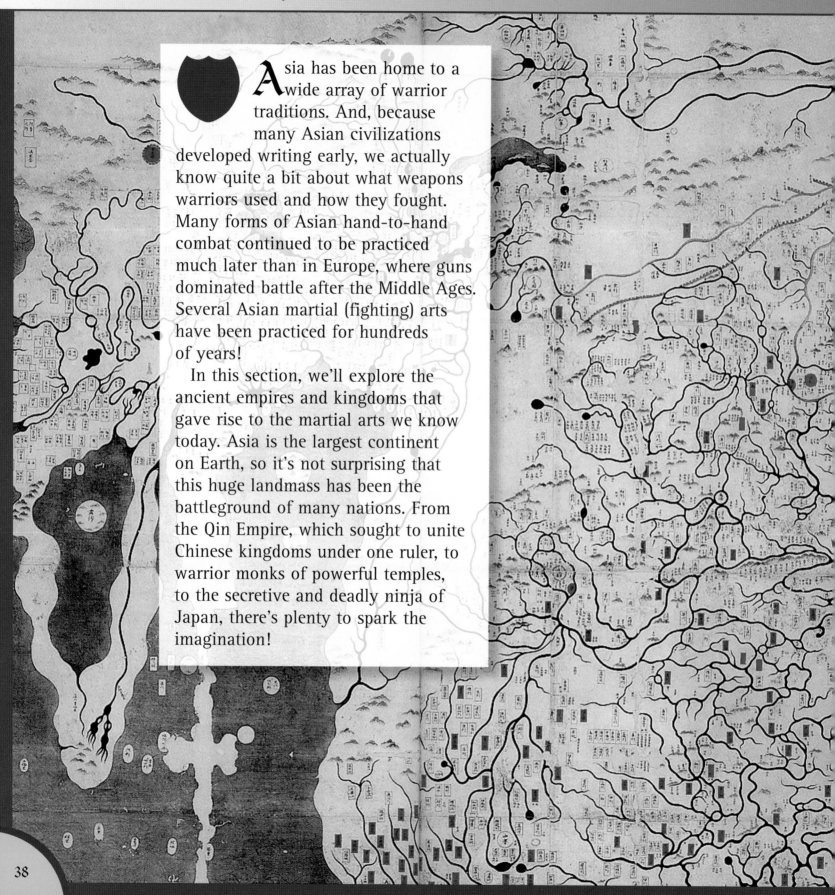

Warriors of Asia

Asia has been home to a wide array of warrior traditions. And, because many Asian civilizations developed writing early, we actually know quite a bit about what weapons warriors used and how they fought. Many forms of Asian hand-to-hand combat continued to be practiced much later than in Europe, where guns dominated battle after the Middle Ages. Several Asian martial (fighting) arts have been practiced for hundreds of years!

In this section, we'll explore the ancient empires and kingdoms that gave rise to the martial arts we know today. Asia is the largest continent on Earth, so it's not surprising that this huge landmass has been the battleground of many nations. From the Qin Empire, which sought to unite Chinese kingdoms under one ruler, to warrior monks of powerful temples, to the secretive and deadly ninja of Japan, there's plenty to spark the imagination!

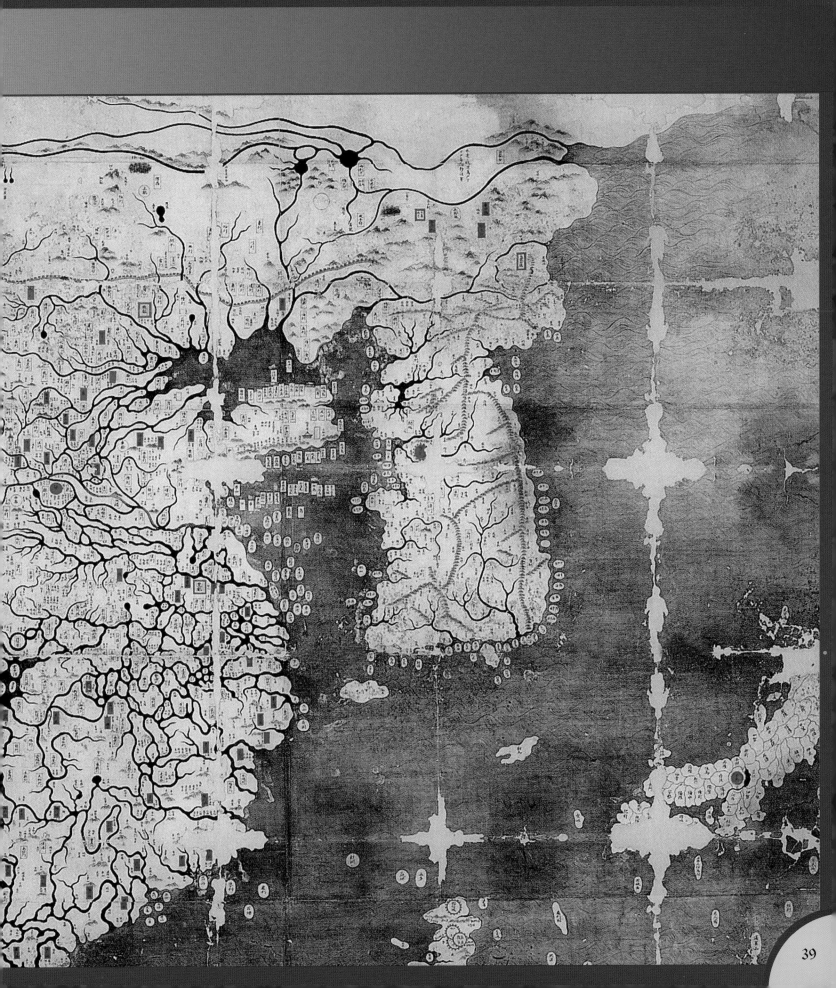

All Under Heaven

The Qin (pronounced "Chin") dynasty ruled for a short time at the end of the third century BCE. Although the Qin Empire lasted only 14 years, it unified the different kingdoms of China, and so the China we know today was largely shaped by the Qin more than 2,000 years ago!

The Qin rose to power during the Warring States period (480–221 BCE) in China, a time of bloody wars between seven main kingdoms. Through strict legal and military organization, the Qin united the warring states. The traditional Chinese view of empire claims that its leader rules "All Under Heaven," or the entire world.

A terracotta warrior from the tomb of Qin Shi Huangdi. This one is an archer and would have been holding a crossbow.

An Army of Clay

THE FIRST QIN EMPEROR was buried with thousands of life-sized statues of warriors. These are known as the "Terracotta Army" because they are made of terracotta clay. A lot of what we know about Qin armor, weaponry, and even military organization comes from these statues.

Unifying China

The first emperor of Qin—Qin Shi Huangdi—unified China in more ways than one. Previously, each territory had its own version of writing, its own money, and its own standards of axle width on carts. Because roads were built to fit the cart, different axle

There are more than 8,000 warriors in the Terracotta Army—and each one has his own unique facial features.

widths meant that only certain carts could be used in certain regions. After conquering China, the Qin emperor standardized all of these. Under the Qin, there was only one form of writing, one type of money, and one axle width throughout the land.

Book Burning

Qin Shi Huangdi and the Qin Empire were famous for their ruthlessness. The emperor took standardization too far when he tried to make everyone follow the same rules and ideas as the Qin. He burned any book that contained different rules or ideas—along with the scholars who knew those books by heart.

WAR CHEST

WEAPONS: Bows, crossbows, iron-tipped spears, swords, chariots

SIEGE WEAPONS: Catapults, siege crossbows

ARMOR: Scale, lamellar, or plate armor of leather, bronze, or iron; helmets of leather or bronze; wooden shields

FORTIFICATIONS: Stone and rammed earth castles, walls, and forts

LOCATION: Northern China

TIME PERIOD: 221 to 207 BCE

MAIN ENEMIES: Rebels from the previous warring states and nomads from the steppes

DID YOU KNOW?

The Qin built the first Great Wall to protect northern China from nomadic tribes. The original Great Wall was built of stone and rammed earth, a mixture of clay and sand packed tightly into shape.

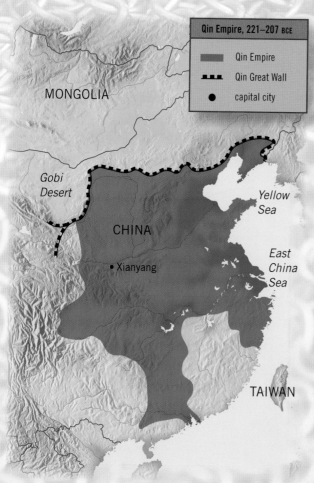

Qin Empire, 221–207 BCE

- Qin Empire
- Qin Great Wall
- capital city

MONGOLIA

Gobi Desert

CHINA

• Xianyang

Yellow Sea

East China Sea

TAIWAN

A section of the Great Wall as it stands today. This section was built during the Ming Dynasty (1368–1644). Including natural barriers such as hills, the Great Wall runs for about 5,500 miles.

Horsemen of the Steppes

In the thirteenth century CE, the Mongols conquered a huge portion of the world and created the largest ancient or medieval empire ever. The Mongol Empire covered more than 12,700,000 square miles—an area larger than the entire continent of Africa. The Mongols invaded Japan in the east and made it all the way to Hungary and Poland in the west.

The core of Mongol military power was the horse archer. Mongols lived as nomads (wandering herdsmen) on the steppes (flat, dry land) north of China. Always on the move, Mongols grew up riding horses and hunting with bows. Any male old enough to shoot a bow and under the age of 60 was required to serve in the military. That meant that nearly the entire male population could be mobilized as an army. No one knows for sure how big the Mongol armies were, but estimates start at 100,000 soldiers. Mongol horse archers would each bring several extra horses to battle, and sometimes they would mount dummies on the extra horses. This gave their enemies the impression of a much larger force than the Mongols actually had.

DID YOU KNOW?

Most arrowheads are barbed, which makes them difficult to remove from flesh. To remove an arrow, someone has to cut it out or push it all the way through the body. The Mongols, however, wore silk beneath their armor. When an arrow strikes someone wearing silk, the arrow still goes into the flesh of the warrior, but does not break the silk. This makes it possible to take out barbed arrows by tugging at the silk around the wound, minimizing damage to the warrior.

Riding tough horses from Central Asia, the Mongols were fast, disciplined, and organized.

WAR CHEST

WEAPONS: Composite bows, swords, axes, lances

SIEGE WEAPONS: Catapults, trebuchets

ARMOR: Scale or plate armor of leather, iron, or steel with silk underneath; steel helmets; round shields

FORTIFICATIONS: Mongols had no fortresses of their own, but used those native to the lands they conquered.

LOCATION: Based in Mongolia, but spreading east to Japan, west through Russia to Poland and Austria, and south to India, Persia, and Iraq

TIME PERIOD: 1206 to 1368 CE

MAIN ENEMIES: Jin Dynasty China, Persians, Arabs, Russians, Hungarians, Poles, Turks

RULERS OF THE STEPPES

THE TWO GREATEST LEADERS of the Mongols were Genghis Khan (also known as Temujin) and his grandson Kublai Khan. Both of them were known for being ruthless to enemies but tolerant as rulers. Kublai Khan was raised by his mother, an extremely powerful queen named Sorghaghtani Beki. She made sure Kublai trained in archery and learned to read and write. Kublai allowed local customs, traditions, and beliefs to continue in the places he conquered. Kublai had Christian, Buddhist, and Muslim advisers in his court.

Genghis Khan

Queen Sorghaghtani Beki

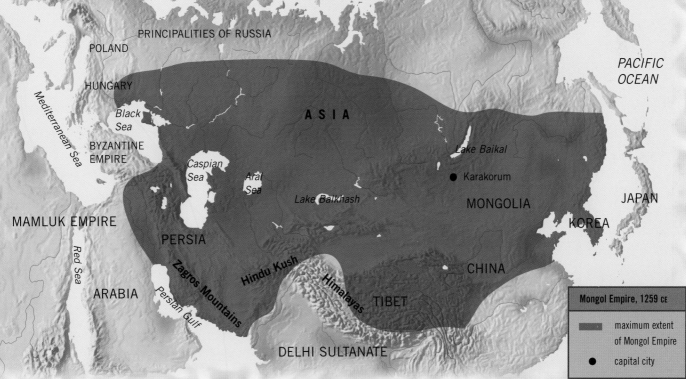

PRINCIPALITIES OF RUSSIA

POLAND

HUNGARY

Mediterranean Sea

Black Sea

BYZANTINE EMPIRE

Caspian Sea

Aral Sea

A S I A

Lake Baikal

● Karakorum

Lake Balkhash

PACIFIC OCEAN

MAMLUK EMPIRE

PERSIA

Red Sea

Zagros Mountains

Hindu Kush

Persian Gulf

Himalayas

MONGOLIA

KOREA

JAPAN

CHINA

TIBET

ARABIA

DELHI SULTANATE

Mongol Empire, 1259 CE	
	maximum extent of Mongol Empire
●	capital city

The Delhi Sultanate was an Islamic kingdom in northern India. It is called a sultanate because its leader was known as a sultan. The Delhi Sultanate lasted more than three centuries, but Hindu military leaders finally overthrew it and replaced it with the Mughal Empire.

The people of India have employed war elephants for thousands of years. Here, a sixteenth-century Indian emperor and his army cross the Ganges River atop war elephants and horses.

Slave King

The Delhi Sultanate began when the Ghurids—a Persian people of central Asia—conquered a large portion of India. Under the leadership of Muhammad Ghori, a governor of Ghazni in modern-day Afghanistan, the Ghurids defeated the native Rajputs in 1192 CE. After Muhammad Ghori died in 1206, one of his Turkish slave commanders, Qutb-ud-din-Aybak, took control of the Indian territories and set up the Delhi Sultanate.

Strength in Diversity

Because the Delhi Sultanate included many different peoples and ethnicities, it used various fighting styles in combination. The Ghurids traditionally fought on foot, but the Turks in the army were skilled horse archers. Heavily armed cavalry with lances also made up a large part of the army. The skillful combination of these three groups allowed the Ghurids to defeat the Rajputs. Many of the same fighting techniques were maintained throughout much of the sultanate's reign.

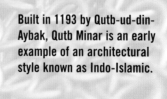

Built in 1193 by Qutb-ud-din-Aybak, Qutb Minar is an early example of an architectural style known as Indo-Islamic.

WAR CHEST

WEAPONS: Bows and arrows, lances, spears, swords, war elephants

ARMOR: Chain mail or scale armor, steel helmets, shields of rawhide and cotton padding

FORTIFICATIONS: Strengthened existing fortifications in northern India of stone and earth

LOCATION: Northern India

TIME PERIOD: 1192 to 1526 CE

MAIN ENEMIES: Rajputs, Mongols, Hindu rebels

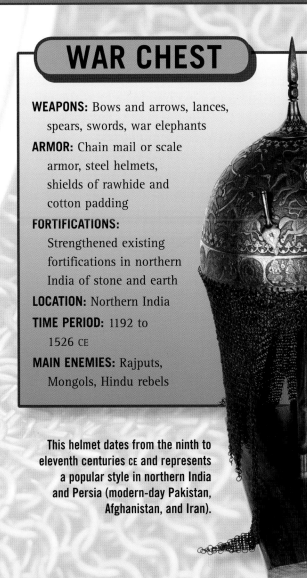

This helmet dates from the ninth to eleventh centuries CE and represents a popular style in northern India and Persia (modern-day Pakistan, Afghanistan, and Iran).

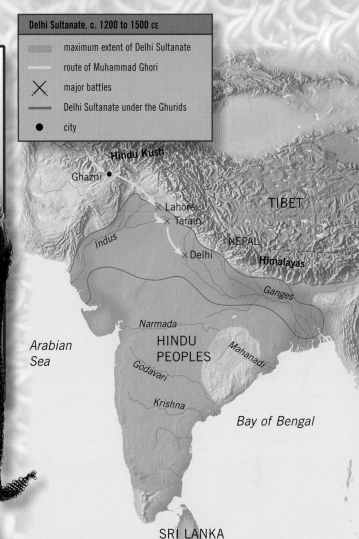

Delhi Sultanate, c. 1200 to 1500 CE

- maximum extent of Delhi Sultanate
- route of Muhammad Ghori
- ✕ major battles
- Delhi Sultanate under the Ghurids
- ● city

Hindu Kush

Ghazni ●

Lahore
Tarain

TIBET

Indus

NEPAL

Delhi

Himalayas

Narmada

Ganges

Arabian Sea

HINDU PEOPLES

Mahanadi

Godavari

Krishna

Bay of Bengal

SRI LANKA

Protected by Land and Sea

OVER TIME, the sultanate grew to cover almost the entire Indian subcontinent. The Delhi Sultanate was one of few kingdoms to successfully defend itself against the Mongol hordes. Geography helped them in this: India is protected from the north by the Himalayas and from the east and west by seas. Only a few mountain passes provide access to India by land. Even with the natural fortification of the northern mountains, however, the Mongols presented a serious threat to the Delhi Sultanate.

DID YOU KNOW?

Razia Sultana—or Razia the Sultan—ruled for a short time, from 1236 to 1240. She was one of the very few female leaders of an early Islamic culture. As sultan, Razia was commander of the armies and fought against the Mongols. She wore male clothing and showed her face in public, something that other noble women could not do.

The Sword of Heaven

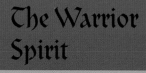

Religious figures in East Asia have a long and illustrious history as warriors. From mountain monks who terrorized Japan to the legendary heroes of Shaolin Temple, few groups of warriors have played with the imagination more than the warrior monks of East Asia. Known for their rigorous discipline, strength, and skill, these monks developed fighting arts shrouded in the mystery of ancient spiritual traditions.

Traveling Monks

Most warrior monks in East Asia were Buddhist, though some practiced Taoism or other religions. In Japan, warrior priests were called *sōhei* ("monk soldiers") and held significant political power from the eighth century CE onward. Alongside the *sōhei* were the *yamabushi* ("mountain warriors"), who lived and traveled alone. Monks often traveled great distances and had to defend themselves from thieves and bandits along the road. They also had to defend the relics and shrines of their temples. For these reasons, nearly every monastery or group of warrior monks had its own style of fighting. Korean monks, for example, developed ways of using the sash from their robes to defend against, capture, or kill an opponent.

Bodhidharma, a fifth-century monk from India, is traditionally credited with introducing Buddhism to China and developing Shaolin kung fu.

The Warrior Spirit

WARRIOR MONKS BLENDED their spiritual practice with their practice of martial arts. The rigors of physical training gave monks the discipline they needed for meditation. Meditation likewise helped their fighting skills. The foundation of East Asian martial arts is the concept of an internal energy (called *chi* in Chinese, *ki* in Japanese). Warrior monks sought to use this energy for both martial arts and healing.

Much Chinese landscape painting, such as this example by Wang Meng from the fourteenth century, blends the physical with the spiritual. This impulse stems in part from Chinese Buddhism, and is also reflected in the spiritual/physical practice of martial arts.

A Shaolin monk demonstrates his skill. Known worldwide for their fighting style today, Shaolin monks have been practicing combat since at least the eighth century.

WACKIEST WEAPONS OF THE WARRIOR MONKS

1. *Three-sectional staff:* A Chinese weapon made from three short staves connected by chains

2. *Rope dart:* The rope dart is a heavy metal spike on the end of a long rope. A skilled practitioner can spin the rope and shoot the dart with piercing force and accuracy.

3. *Monk's spade:* A long pole with a shovel-shaped blade on one end and a crescent-shaped blade on the other

4. *Belt or sash:* Always at hand, a monk's belt could be used to block weapons, twist or break joints, bind in capture, or suffocate an opponent.

5. *Fingertips:* Several styles of East Asian martial arts train the fingertips to become incredibly strong. A skilled warrior can injure, knock unconscious, or even kill an opponent with a single strike.

A *naginata*, a weapon used by *sōhei* warriors of Japan beginning in the eighth century

Chinese throwing darts

Kings of the Jungles

In the late eighth century CE, a prince from Java called Jayavarman II conquered and united many small kingdoms in Southeast Asia. In 802 Jayavarman declared himself emperor of Khmer (pronounced "Ka-mer") and began building the city of Angkor, the pride of the empire. Eventually, the Khmer Empire grew to cover much of the region, including modern-day Cambodia, Thailand, Myanmar (Burma), and parts of Malaysia.

Living Siege Weapons

The Khmer relied heavily on the war elephant. The Asian elephant can stand up to 12 feet tall, weigh up to 11,000 pounds, and charge upward of 20 miles per hour. Imagine an entire army of war elephants charging at full speed! The elephants could trample and crush enemies like few other engines of war and sometimes carried siege crossbows into battle. The Khmer also used horses and warships. Archers and martial artists, sometimes trained in combat by Buddhist monks, rounded out the Khmer army.

DID YOU KNOW?

Khmer warriors made shields out of rhinoceros skin, which can grow to two inches thick.

A carving showing a battle between the Khmer and the Cham, an enemy to the east

Feeding the Army

ONE OF THE REASONS the Khmer Empire flourished was successful management of farming and irrigation (using canals and other man-made structures to bring water to dry areas). Southeast Asia gets a lot of rain during the rainy season, but the rivers and lakes dry up quickly during the dry season. Khmer kings built reservoirs to store water and maintained canals. This allowed the Khmer to produce lots of rice, which the army needed to survive. Without this careful use of the environment, all the might of the Khmer army would have been useless.

The jungle has largely reclaimed the Khmer capital of Angkor, adding to its mystique. Here, a tree has grown over the stones of Ta Prohm, a temple near Angkor Wat.

Khmer Empire, 1200 CE

- Champa
- Khmer Empire
- ● capital city

MYANMAR (BURMA)

LAOS

VIETNAM

Salween

Mekong

THAILAND

Bay of Bengal

● Angkor

CAMBODIA

South China Sea

RELIGION AND WAR

AT FIRST, the Khmer Empire worshipped Hindu gods. Over time, however, the Khmer became more Buddhist than Hindu. For example, the most famous temple of the Khmer, Angkor Wat, was originally Hindu and then converted to Buddhist use. Buddhism brought more than new religious practices, however. As in China, forms of hand-to-hand combat were practiced and taught by Buddhist warrior monks.

The warrior monks heavily influenced Khmer fighting techniques. Some of these techniques may survive today in modern Southeast Asian boxing and wrestling sports. A modern martial artist's strike with the knee can deliver as much force as a car driving at 30 miles per hour!

Angkor Wat, the most famous temple of the Khmer Empire

The Life-Giving Sword

The samurai were the warrior class of Japan from the Heian period (794–1185 CE) until the late nineteenth century, when methods of modern warfare supplanted them. The age of the samurai ended when the warriors were no longer allowed to wear their swords. The samurai saw his sword as not just a weapon, but as his soul. This concept is the basis of *The Life-Giving Sword*, a famous seventeenth-century book on swordsmanship by Yagyu Munenori.

Samurai swords were single-edged and slightly curved, making them stronger and more efficient in use on horseback. Talented smiths made samurai swords out of many layers of steel. The core of the sword was relatively soft to absorb blows, but the edge was extremely hard and razor sharp. Because swords were so important to this military elite, famous sword makers sometimes became legendary themselves.

Samurai actually carried two swords. The longer, primary sword of the samurai was a *katana*. The second and shorter sword was known as a *wakizashi*. Sometimes warriors used both in battle, but the *wakizashi* was not used in fighting as much. Instead, warriors used it to commit ritual suicide—called hara-kiri—if they had lost their honor.

Samurai sometimes tested the quality of a sword on the bodies of criminals. Diagrams from medieval Japan show 16 different cuts that could be made through the body. The most difficult—which only the best swords could make—was straight across the hips.

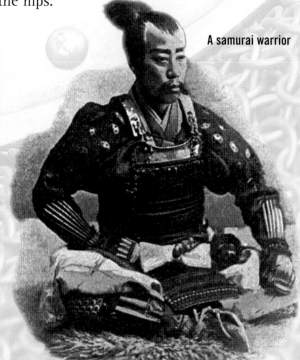

A samurai warrior

GREAT SWORDSMAN

ONE OF THE most famous samurai was named Miyamoto Musashi. Often traveling and training alone in the wilderness, Musashi dedicated himself completely to the perfection of his swordsmanship. Although not the first to use both swords, Musashi is famous for fighting with both the long and short swords. He won more than 60 duels. Today, he is best known for his book on swordsmanship, called *A Book of Five Rings*.

Miyamoto Musashi

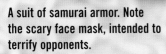

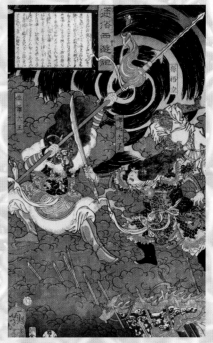

A legendary battle between two samurai fighting with a *naginata* (left) and a *katana* (right)

Protect and Terrify

SAMURAI MADE THEIR ARMOR out of many materials, including iron, silk, and plates of lacquered leather. Constructed to terrify opponents, Japanese armor was never designed to withstand direct blows—the samurai relied on skill to avoid direct hits. Samurai trained to run, jump, ride, and swim in full armor. There were even entire schools of swordsmanship for teaching how to fight in the water.

A suit of samurai armor. Note the scary face mask, intended to terrify opponents.

WAR CHEST

WEAPONS: Single-edged swords called *katana*; spears; pole weapons called *naginata*; bows and arrows

ARMOR: Scale or plate armor of iron and lacquered leather, helmets of iron with face masks made to look as scary as possible

FORTIFICATIONS: Large stone castles

LOCATION: Japan

TIME PERIOD: About 800 to 1900 CE

MAIN ENEMIES: Koreans, Chinese, and Mongols, but mostly each other

A *katana* and its leather sheath

Warriors of the Shadows

Ninja are the stuff of legend. They developed in the late sixth or early seventh century in Japan, and a few exist even today. Assassins, spies, and soldiers, the ninja were elite warriors. With cunning, trickery, and technology—as well as intense physical training—ninja performed seemingly impossible feats of strength and stealth.

In past times, ninja were a well-defined class of society. They even participated openly, alongside samurai, in large battles. Often seen as outsiders of society, ninja mostly lived in the mountains of Iga and Koga provinces in central Japan. They lived as warriors and farmers, and even young children practiced the ninja's secret arts. Every weapon made by ninja could also be used as a tool. The scabbard of the ninja's sword, for example, could function as a snorkel, allowing the ninja to breathe under water.

The folk hero Ishikawa Goemon (top) prepares his assassination attempt on Toyotomi Hideyoshi (bottom) in his castle. Ninja developed numerous techniques for sneaking up on their powerful opponents.

Deadly Masquerade

Contrary to popular belief, ninja wore their dark hooded suits only on special night missions. Most of the time, they pretended to be someone else: a traveling entertainer, a Buddhist priest, a humble farmer. Female ninja—known as *kunoichi*—were particularly good at pretending to be harmless women, only to reveal their true deadly natures at the right moments.

DID YOU KNOW?
Ninja developed special methods of side walking so that someone tracking them could not tell which direction they were traveling.

The popular image of a ninja today

FUNKIEST WEAPONS OF THE NINJA

1. *Kamagusari:* A sickle with a chain attached to the handle and a weight on the end of the chain
2. *Shuko:* Claws strapped onto the hand to help in climbing trees and walls—also nasty weapons
3. *Blowgun:* A hollow pipe used to shoot darts, often with poisoned tips
4. *Manrikigusari:* A chain with a weighted spike on either end. The chain could block sword blows or bind and strangle an opponent, while the weighted ends could be thrown like darts.
5. *Blinding powder:* A powder that could be thrown into an opponent's face to temporarily blind him or her

A throwing star, or *shuriken*, a type of concealed weapon that ninjas have used from the sixteenth century or earlier

PACIFIC OCEAN

Sea of Japan

JAPAN

Tokyo ●

Lake Biwa

Philippine Sea

Japan	
	Shiga prefecture
	Mie prefecture

The mountains of Iga and Koga, now in Mie and Shiga prefectures in central Japan, once housed several ninja communities.

Chirping Floors

AS MASTERS OF STEALTH, ninja often snuck into palaces to spy on or assassinate important officials. They practiced walking on all fours, which kept their footfalls light and silent on these secret missions. But some powerful lords had special flooring installed in their castles that would squeak or chirp when someone walked on it. This would let the palace inhabitants know if ninja were attacking.

WAR CHEST

WEAPONS: Single-edged straight swords, spears, bows and arrows, shuriken, blowguns, caltrops, explosives, poison, chain and sickles, nunchaku, sai, staves, and more!

ARMOR: Usually no armor, unless the ninja were posing as samurai or soldiers. They may have used a lightweight armor that could have been worn under their dark clothing.

FORTIFICATIONS: None

LOCATION: Japan

TIME PERIOD: Seventh century CE to the present day

MAIN ENEMIES: Whoever ninja were paid to kill, or whoever had done them wrong

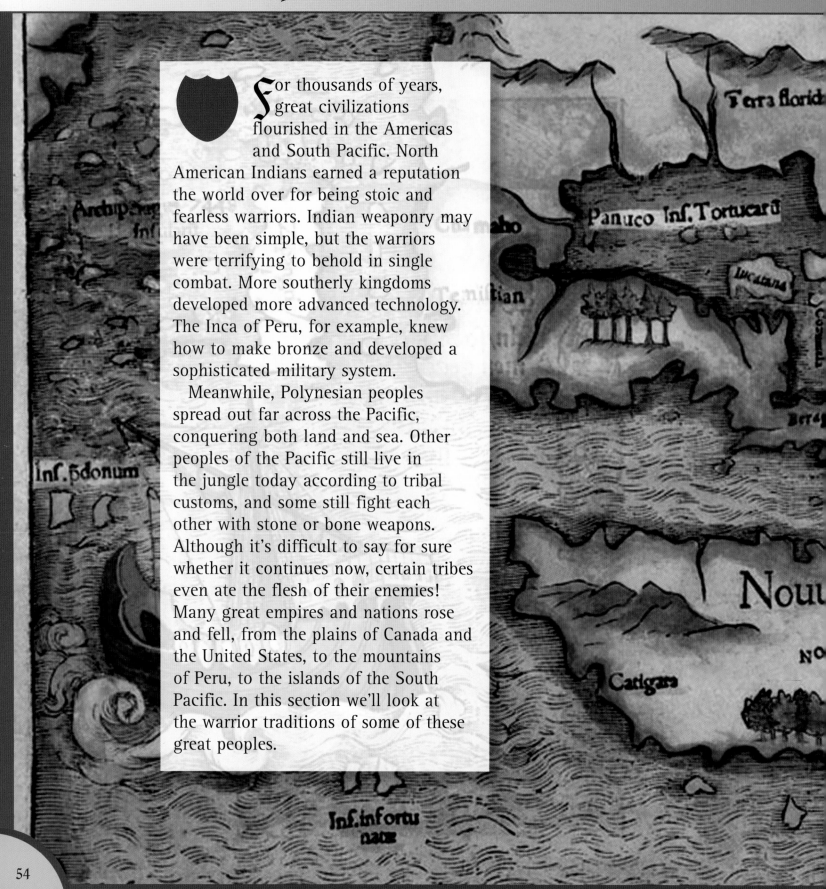

Warriors of the New World

For thousands of years, great civilizations flourished in the Americas and South Pacific. North American Indians earned a reputation the world over for being stoic and fearless warriors. Indian weaponry may have been simple, but the warriors were terrifying to behold in single combat. More southerly kingdoms developed more advanced technology. The Inca of Peru, for example, knew how to make bronze and developed a sophisticated military system.

Meanwhile, Polynesian peoples spread out far across the Pacific, conquering both land and sea. Other peoples of the Pacific still live in the jungle today according to tribal customs, and some still fight each other with stone or bone weapons. Although it's difficult to say for sure whether it continues now, certain tribes even ate the flesh of their enemies! Many great empires and nations rose and fell, from the plains of Canada and the United States, to the mountains of Peru, to the islands of the South Pacific. In this section we'll look at the warrior traditions of some of these great peoples.

Excel...
Hispania

Oceanus occidentalis

CVBA
Hispaniola

Antilla
Inf. Hesp.

Sciant.

Iamica
Dominica
S. Iacobi

AFRICAE
pars

PARIA Sabundat
auro & margarites

orbis

...ula Atlantica quam uo/
...nt Brasilij & Americam.

Canibali

Sinus
Atlanticus

Die Nüw
Welt

In the Mountains of Peru

The Inca created one of the greatest empires in the Americas. Today, many Inca monuments still stand in the Andes Mountains. The most famous of these ruins is Machu Picchu, most likely a royal citadel built toward the end of the fifteenth century CE.

The Incas' skill as builders helped them become a military superpower, because their huge network of roads allowed scouts, messengers, and armies to travel quickly over large distances. The Incan road system allowed messages to be transported quickly, and shelters, maintained by the empire along the road, ensured that marching armies would always have a handy place to stay the night and grab a meal.

DID YOU KNOW?

Inca warriors used long-distance projectile weapons before closing in with lances and clubs. Though they used bows and arrows, it seems they preferred the sling and stone. Slings are easy to make, and ammunition was always at hand in the rocky mountains. Though difficult to master, slings can be incredibly accurate.

Test of Fear

The empire required all able-bodied males to perform military service. This meant that the Inca could raise a large army quickly. Boys trained to fight from about the age of 10 to about the age of 18. At the end of their training, they were often tested by being told they were going to be killed. If they showed any fear when the executioner raised his weapon, they were deemed unworthy to be part of the elite army.

A sling from the Andes, made out of the hair of a llama, a beast of burden domesticated by the Inca

A statue of the last Incan king, Atahualpa, stands in Cuzco, Peru. First captured, then executed by Spanish invaders, Atahualpa died in 1533.

WAR CHEST

WEAPONS: Slings and stones, bolas, bronze-tipped spears, spear throwers, lances, bows and arrows, clubs, wooden swords of palm wood

ARMOR: Wooden and/or leather helmets, cotton padding on the body with metal breastplates, small round shields of palm wood and cotton padding

FORTIFICATIONS: Stone hill forts called *pucaras*, walls, and palaces

LOCATION: The Andes Mountains of South America, mostly in modern-day Peru

TIME PERIOD: Sixth century to about the sixteenth century CE

MAIN ENEMIES: Most names unknown, but all the tribes of the Andes, especially ones with good farmland. Later, Spanish conquistadors

A bola, which could be thrown with great force to cripple or kill an opponent

TUPAC INCA

TUPAC INCA was one of the last great Inca kings. He ruled from 1471 to 1493. A great military leader and strategist, Tupac Inca inspired his followers to great feats. When blocked by a swamp, he put his army to work—joining in the labor himself—and they built a stone and earth causeway across the swamp in only a few days. Tupac Inca is also said to have explored a part of the Pacific Ocean, most likely on a balsa wood raft. Some claim he made it to the Galapagos Islands, while others claim his voyage took him to Easter Island, far out in the Pacific.

The Inca Empire, 1438–1525

	maximum extent of the Inca Empire
	Incan roads
●	Incan settlement

The ruins of Machu Picchu are among the most spectacular buildings of pre-Columbian (before Christopher Columbus) South America.

From the Mountains to the Prairies

The Sioux (pronounced "Sue") roamed the Rocky Mountains and the Great Plains as one of the great American Indian tribes of the North American West. Living in tipis, hunting bison, and wearing eagle feather headdresses, the Sioux survived as fearless warriors and expert woodsmen.

The Sioux lived in tipis. These could be quickly taken down and easily carried, which allowed the Sioux to follow the herds of bison that they hunted.

A Hard-Knock Life

Training for the Sioux warrior started early. Children were taught to endure hardship without complaint, even if this meant going without food for days. Children were often expected to demonstrate their hardiness, perhaps by breaking a hole in the ice and swimming in a frozen lake during the winter. Full warriors proved themselves by running an entire day and night without stopping. The young Sioux warrior learned to track game, navigate huge stretches of forest, find food and herbs for medicine, and perform all the necessary duties of daily life. This training also honed the warrior's mind to the ever-present danger of enemy attack. Sioux warriors would begin going to war usually in their mid- to late teens.

Going to War

The Sioux's main enemies were the United States Army and the Ojibwe Indians. The Ojibwe used similar weaponry and underwent similar training as the Sioux. Both Indian groups fought with short-range bows made of osage orange wood, lances tipped with stone or bone blades, clubs weighted with

stone, and shields of rawhide. Arrows were tipped with stone or bone. Once Europeans introduced horses to North America, the Sioux warrior became a skilled equestrian and usually rode bareback. Some Sioux could even shoot arrows while riding underneath the belly of the horse, just holding on with their feet!

THE MASSACRE OF WOUNDED KNEE

ON DECEMBER 29, 1890, U.S. forces cornered the last band of Sioux warriors at Wounded Knee Creek in South Dakota. The army instructed the Sioux to hand over their weapons, but in the confusion, a shot was fired. The American soldiers opened fire on the Sioux, killing 300 men, women, and children in what is now known as the Massacre of Wounded Knee. Many of the Sioux killed were "Ghost Dancers," warriors who participated in a frenzied dance and wore special shirts that they believed bullets couldn't penetrate. Sadly, bullets did indeed pierce the shirts, and the massacre largely put an end to Sioux resistance against the U.S. Army.

WAR CHEST

WEAPONS: Bows and arrows; lances tipped with stone points; tomahawks, war clubs

ARMOR: Round shields made from two layers of rawhide, taken from the neck of a bison

FORTIFICATIONS: None

LOCATION: The Rocky Mountains and Great Plains of the northern United States and Canada

TIME PERIOD: Sometime before the seventeenth century CE to the present day

MAIN ENEMIES: Ojibwe, white settlers, the U.S. Army

A Sioux warrior. The Sioux's last great victory came in 1876, when they handed a major defeat to United States general George Custer at the Battle of Little Bighorn in Montana.

A Sioux war dance

In the Forests of the East

The Iroquois lived primarily in upstate New York, but stretched north into Canada and south into Ohio and Pennsylvania. Five tribes, known as the Five Nations, made up the Iroquois Confederacy: the Mohawk, Oneida, Onondaga, Cayuga, and Seneca. The Tuscarora joined the confederacy later.

DID YOU KNOW?

According to legend, a man known as the Great Peacemaker united the Five Nations of the Iroquois. Hiawatha, a great speaker, helped him achieve this unity. Hiawatha is one of the most celebrated names in Iroquoian history.

People of the Longhouse

Although no one knows for sure, the term *Iroquois* might mean "killers." Hostile Indians might have given them this name. The Iroquois call themselves *Haudenosaunee* ("Ho-deh-no-shaw-nee"), meaning "people of the longhouse," because they lived in longhouses covered with bark, usually from birch trees. Each longhouse had a central aisle and apartments organized by family on either side. Longhouses could be more than 300 feet long. Palisades (high timber fences) with trenches outside often surrounded villages.

Prisoner of War

The Iroquois were dedicated warriors and became staunch allies of the British during the French and Indian War (1754–1763). This is also called the Seven Years War. During the American Revolutionary War (1775–1783), members of the Confederacy fought on both sides, causing violent internal strife.

Iroquois warriors took heads or scalps as trophies of war. Captives were taken back

An Iroquois warrior decorates a monument in Montreal, Canada.

An Iroquois longhouse

to the village, where they were sometimes incorporated into the tribe. Taking captives was seen as a way of replacing fallen comrades and family members. If captives were not adopted, they were often brutally tortured and killed.

Game of War

LACROSSE WAS A GAME invented and played by Indians from many different tribes. The Iroquois played lacrosse not just for entertainment, but also to train warriors for battle and even to resolve conflicts without actually fighting. Indians called it *baggataway*, which means "the little brother of war." Iroquois lacrosse games were very different from their modern version: there was no padded equipment, scores were low, there could be several hundred players on one team, and the field could be a mile long!

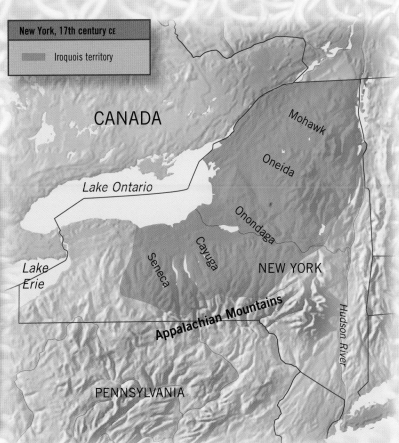

New York, 17th century CE

Iroquois territory

CANADA

Mohawk

Oneida

Lake Ontario

Onondaga

Cayuga

Lake Erie

Seneca

NEW YORK

Appalachian Mountains

Hudson River

PENNSYLVANIA

A painting of an Indian lacrosse game

WAR CHEST

WEAPONS: Bows and arrows, spears tipped with stone points, blowguns, tomahawks, war clubs

ARMOR: Shields, breastplates made from strips of wood or bone

FORTIFICATIONS: Wood stockades and trenches

LOCATION: Northeast United States and southern Canada, primarily in upstate New York

TIME PERIOD: Fifteenth century CE to the present day

MAIN ENEMIES: Huron, Algonquin tribes, white settlers

Bone Breakers

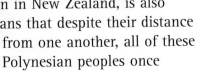

Even though they are separated by thousands and thousands of miles of open ocean, native Hawaiians and Tahitians (in French Polynesia) speak almost the same language. The Maori language, spoken in New Zealand, is also similar. This means that despite their distance from one another, all of these Polynesian peoples once came from the same place and spoke the same language, indicating that they were excellent sailors.

The Hawaiians built splendid canoes from native koa trees. If desired, two canoes could connect to create a catamaran. These big ships could be up to 100 feet long. Warriors often sailed on the warpath, beaching in enemy territory to begin the battle. Lookouts were therefore important for the safety of the Hawaiian tribes.

Now a national historic park, Pu'ohona o Hōnaunau once offered sanctuary to Hawaiians in need, including defeated warriors and women and children who wished to avoid bloodshed.

Weapons of Hawaii

Hawaiian warriors favored spears and clubs. Battles usually began with a volley of stones, either thrown by hand or by slings. Then warriors would close in with hardwood spears, which were often more than 13 feet long. Hawaiians also made clubs out of hardwood and often attached a stone to the end. For very close range, Hawaiians used a variety of daggers made from wood or bone. Perhaps the most brutal Hawaiian weapon was the shark-tooth club—a flat, paddlelike club with shark teeth set around the edge. The teeth could cut an enemy viciously or break off and embed in the flesh.

Royal Wrestling

Even though Hawaiians had a range of weapons, some warriors preferred to fight with their bare hands. The Hawaiian method of hand-to-hand combat is called *Lua*, which was taught only to Hawaiian royalty.

THE LAST VOYAGE OF CAPTAIN COOK

IN 1778, CAPTAIN JAMES COOK became the first European explorer to reach the Hawaiian Islands. Cook had already been to New Zealand and Tahiti, so he was familiar with the Polynesian language and culture. For the most part, Cook found the Hawaiians to be extremely generous and kind; however, on a return voyage, some Hawaiian natives tried to steal a boat from Cook's crew. In the resulting skirmish, Hawaiian warriors killed Cook. He first took a blow to the back of the head with a club, then was stabbed and beaten to death.

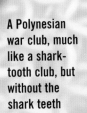

A Polynesian war club, much like a shark-tooth club, but without the shark teeth

Lua is a no-nonsense fighting system: it's all about locking joints and breaking bones. By skillful control of an opponent's joints, Hawaiian warriors used both their own and their opponent's body weight to deliver crushing injuries.

Polynesia is a large area of the Pacific Ocean, covering more than 1,000 islands and some 10 million square miles. Not all of the islands in the "Polynesian Triangle" are inhabited, but on those that are, the people speak a Polynesian language. No one knows for sure how these seafaring peoples managed to cross such large distances of open ocean without the benefits of any modern technology, but Polynesians probably came from Southeast Asia about 5,000 years ago and gradually spread east, reaching Hawaii by 500 CE.

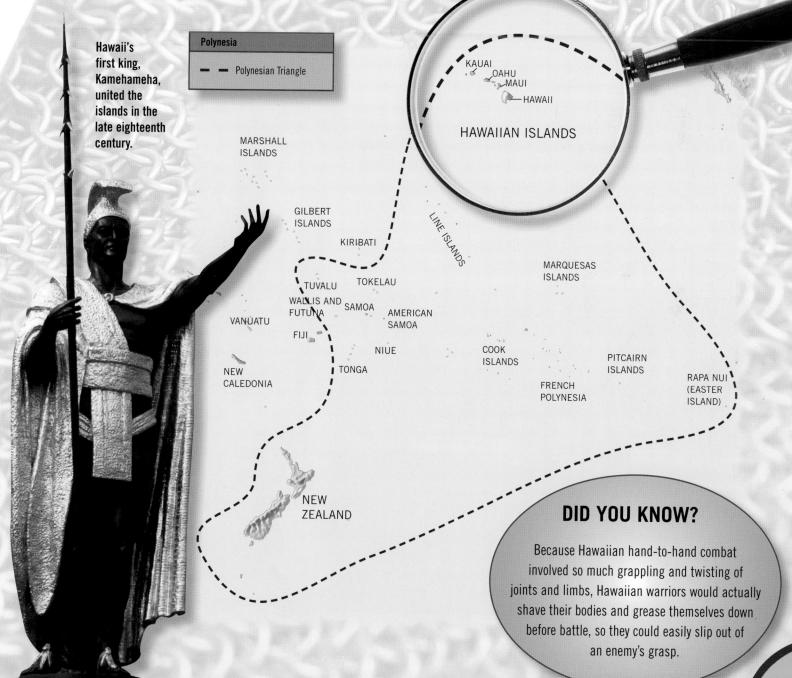

Hawaii's first king, Kamehameha, united the islands in the late eighteenth century.

Polynesia

– – Polynesian Triangle

KAUAI
OAHU
MAUI
HAWAII
HAWAIIAN ISLANDS

MARSHALL ISLANDS

GILBERT ISLANDS

KIRIBATI

LINE ISLANDS

MARQUESAS ISLANDS

TUVALU
TOKELAU
WALLIS AND FUTUNA
SAMOA
AMERICAN SAMOA

VANUATU

FIJI

NIUE

COOK ISLANDS

PITCAIRN ISLANDS

NEW CALEDONIA

TONGA

FRENCH POLYNESIA

RAPA NUI (EASTER ISLAND)

NEW ZEALAND

DID YOU KNOW?

Because Hawaiian hand-to-hand combat involved so much grappling and twisting of joints and limbs, Hawaiian warriors would actually shave their bodies and grease themselves down before battle, so they could easily slip out of an enemy's grasp.

Sea Warriors of New Zealand

The Maori probably came to New Zealand from the east around the year 1000 CE. Maori legend places their original homeland in the west, in a place called "Hawaiki," but no one knows for sure where this might be. Using only stone tools, the Maori produced impressive buildings, ships, and elaborately carved artwork. Maori culture is still alive today, and New Zealand sports teams often perform a war dance—called a *haka*—before matches.

Maori warriors favored spears and masterfully carved stone clubs, sharpened on either side. The Maori warrior was called a *toa*. Young boys trained in the arts of war from an early age, and wrestling was a favored sport because it helped prepare children for fighting in battle. Women often accompanied men on war parties, and some may even have taken part in the fighting.

Canoes and Fortresses

The Maori had wonderful war canoes, called *waka*, paddled by dozens of warriors who dipped their oars to the rhythm of a chant sung by a leader onboard. These canoes sometimes had sails and were intricately carved and decorated.

The Maori built fortresses of earth, stone, and wood. The fortress was called a *pa* and had several layers of defense made up of trenches, palisades, and fighting platforms. The Maori shaped entire hills into fortresses—all with only digging sticks and wooden spades!

Carved Polynesian gods, called *tiki*

The Maori war canoe, or *waka*, could carry up to 80 warriors.

Patterns of War

THE MAORI are well known for tattooing their bodies with intricate swirling designs. The patterns can even cover the entire face. Sometimes, the Maori would mummify the head of a dead relative as a keepsake. Some of these mummified heads survive, their facial tattoos still visible.

WAR CHEST

WEAPONS: Spears, staves; long clubs called *pouwhenua*, *tewhatewha*, and *taiaha*; short clubs called *patu*

ARMOR: The Maori usually fought naked, but sometimes wore a tightly woven shirt to protect the torso.

FORTIFICATIONS: Forts known as *pa* made of trenches, earthworks, and palisades

LOCATION: New Zealand

TIME PERIOD: Approximately 1000 CE to the present

MAIN ENEMIES: Other Maori tribes

A Maori war club from the nineteenth century

DID YOU KNOW?

After battles and at times when other meat was scarce, the Maori practiced cannibalism. Feasting on the flesh of enemies was a way of exulting in victory. Sticking out the tongue is an important part of the war dance and sends the message: "I will eat you!"

A traditional Maori dance

Rainforest Warriors

There are thousands of islands in the South Pacific—some big, some quite small—and on some of these islands indigenous (native) peoples who have had little or no contact with the outside world still live. Most of these peoples use stone tools, having no knowledge of metal.

WAR CHEST

WEAPONS: Bows and arrows, spears tipped with stone or bone points

ARMOR: None

FORTIFICATIONS: The Korowai have impressive tree houses high up in the air to protect them from enemies.

LOCATION: Papua New Guinea and the islands of the South Pacific

TIME PERIOD: Unknown origin, up to today

MAIN ENEMIES: Other tribes

The indigenous peoples of the South Pacific use weapons like this *calacula*, from Fiji.

Wars among the peoples of the South Pacific are not usually large, organized affairs. They identify with their families or tribes (organized groups that share a social structure and belief system), so South Pacific peoples usually fight in small skirmishes of a few dozen people, or even one-on-one in individual combat. Most battles occur between enemy families and often continue off-and-on for generations in endless cycles of bloodshed and revenge.

Witch Hunting in New Guinea

Disputes can arise in a number of ways, but among the Korowai, the worst fighting stems from accusations of witchcraft. The Korowai live in the rain forests of Papua on the island of New Guinea. When someone dies unexpectedly—perhaps of illness or by accident—the tribe organizes a witch hunt to find the evil person they hold responsible. The tribe then kills and eats this person. Accusations of witchcraft between tribes can

DID YOU KNOW?

When family members died naturally among the Fayu, their bodies were left in the home to decompose. Tribe members would then smear themselves with the fluid from the decomposing bodies until the corpses were completely dried out! Then they hung up the dried heads as tokens of memory. Imagine the smell!

A head tray from Papua New Guinea, from which two severed heads could hang

cause such violence that whole villages have to be abandoned.

Disappearing in the South Pacific

Many South Pacific tribes are quickly dying out or being swallowed up into larger, more modern societies, especially those that live in areas where they come into frequent contact with the outside world. Even in those places, many people are trying to protect indigenous tribes and allow them to continue living as they have done, even though most people are not comfortable with the practice of cannibalism. Some think, however, that cannibalism even as a wartime practice is dying out, and may already be a thing of the past. Because many South Pacific peoples are so isolated, it is difficult to know for sure.

Revenge Killing

IN 2005, Sabine Kuegler, the daughter of two German missionaries (a foreign traveler who tries to convert people to his or her religion), published a book about her experiences growing up with the Fayu, another tribe of Papua. From the time she was 7 to the time she was 17, Sabine lived with the Fayu, who were constantly at war with other tribes in the area. Killing, however, was based entirely on family relationships—a warrior might seek revenge on the family of somebody who killed someone in his own family. Because Sabine and her family were not related by blood to anyone in the Fayu tribe, they were safe. Some of the Fayu ate the flesh of their enemies, and they used only stone, wood, and bone tools as weapons.

A ship typical of Papua New Guinea from the late nineteenth century

A Korowai village, with houses high in the trees

Find Out More

Words to Know

***assegai* spear.** A type of short spear used by the Zulu

ballista. A type of siege crossbow that shot round stones, used by the Romans

bola. A throwing weapon made of stones tied to both ends of a short rope

caliphate. A kingdom ruled by a caliph

caltrops. Barbs strewn on the ground for horses to step on

cannibalism. The practice of humans eating human flesh

composite bow. A bow made of multiple materials, usually including animal horn and sinew

flail. A weapon made of a handle, a chain, and a spiked metal ball on the end of the chain

Greek fire. A chemical mixture shot from an early flamethrower and capable of burning even on water

haka. The traditional Maori war dance

hara-kiri. The ritual suicide committed by shamed samurai

heraldry. The system of identifying heavily armed knights by means of images, symbols, and crests

javelin. A lightweight throwing spear

kamagusari. A chain and sickle used by ninja

katana. The Japanese samurai long sword

khakhua. A Korowai "witch"

knobkerrie. A type of short club

kunoichi. A female ninja

lamellar. A type of armor using small, overlapping plates of leather or metal

lance. A long and heavy stabbing weapon used from horseback

lorica segmenta. A type of body armor used by the Romans made of overlapping plates

Lua. The Hawaiian martial art of grappling

mace. A clublike weapon with a heavy weight or spiked ball on the end of a handle

mangonel. A type of catapult used during the Crusades

moran. A Masai warrior

motte-and-bailey. A type of castle built by the Normans

nunchaku. A weapon consisting of two wooden sticks connected by a rope or chain

onager. A Roman catapult that took its name from the way it kicked when fired. Onagers are a species of wild donkey.

pa. A Maori fortress

palisade. A wooden fence, used for defense

phalanx. A tight formation using shields to create a defensive barrier

pharaoh. The ruler of ancient Egypt

plate armor. Armor made from plates of iron or steel, characteristic of late medieval Europe

pucara. An Incan hill fort

rammed earth. A type of construction popular in ancient China for making walls by mixing clay and sand

sai. A three-pronged Japanese stabbing weapon

scale armor. A type of armor using small scales of leather or metal sewn onto a backing of some kind

scimitar. A type of curved sword native to Egypt and western Asia

seppuku. A version of hara-kiri in which a friend would help a samurai commit suicide

shield wall. A Germanic formation in which warriors stood shoulder to shoulder, forming a tight wall with their shields

shuko. Hand claws used by ninja for climbing trees and walls as well as for fighting

shuriken. Throwing weapons of the ninja, either straight or star-shaped

sling. A weapon consisting of two strings tied to a pouch used to throw stones

sōhei. Japanese warrior monks

sultanate. A kingdom ruled by a sultan

testudo. The Roman "turtle" formation, in which soldiers used shields to create a defensive wall and roof

toa. A Maori warrior

trebuchet. A siege weapon that used a massive counterweight and sling to throw large stones at castle walls

waka. A Maori canoe

war elephant. An elephant bred and trained to use in war as cavalry mounts and as living siege weapons.

wakizashi. The Japanese samurai short sword

yamabushi. Japanese warrior monks of the mountains

Books to Read

Bingham, Jane. *Encyclopedia of World History.* London: Usborne Books, 2003.

Dixon, Philip. *Knights and Castles.* New York: Simon and Schuster, 2007.

Draeger, Donn, and Robert W. Smith. *Comprehensive Asian Fighting Arts.* New York: Kodansha International, 1981.

Eastman, Charles A. *Indian Boyhood.* New York: Dover Publications, 1971.

Waldman, Carl, and Molly Braun. *Encyclopedia of Native American Tribes.* New York: Facts on File, 2006.

Sims, Leslie, and Jane Chisholm. *Usborne Book of Castles.* London: Usborne Books, 2002.

Web Sites to Visit

http://www.kidpat.com/world-history/index.php

http://www.historyforkids.org/

Index

Credits